"In a lively and engaging style, my good friend Bob Russell presents a welcomed balance between 'health and wealth' preachers and those who tell us to cut up credit cards. Russell drives home the point that for Christians the issue is not so much *how* we handle money, but our *attitude* toward material things. And he directs our attention to the real source of security, the Lord Jesus Christ."

CHUCK COLSON

PRISON FELLOWSHIP MINISTRIES

WASHINGTON, D.C.

"I can't think of a single person who wouldn't benefit from reading this book. Bob Russell has captured the heart of the money issues and spoken to them with uncommon clarity."

BILL HYBELS

SENIOR PASTOR

WILLOW CREEK COMMUNITY CHURCH

"Bob Russell has taken the teachings of the Bible and written the most practical and inspirational book on money management I've ever read. It brings a whole new meaning to Net Worth!"

DAVID C. NOVAK

PRESIDENT AND CHIEF EXECUTIVE

KFC-USA

"Reading Bob Russell's book, *Money: A User's Manual,* is like lowering a bucket into a deep well of advice and drawing up concepts that are clear and refreshing. Also true is that nearly every page of this book is graced with a story or illustration out of real life that makes his advice about dealing with money and possessions both practical and understandable. You can draw from this well and trust that the water is good."

STEVE CHAPMAN

(OF STEVE AND ANNIE CHAPMAN)

GOODLETTESVILLE, TN

"Pastor Bob has taken the emotional feelings about money, spending, envy, and giving and has answered questions most Christians didn't dare to ask. Bob doesn't waste words or your time, so start reading this book today!"

"The devastating effect of materialism on the American family is evident everywhere: debt, divorce, and depression. Even most Christians are preoccupied with the desire to acquire. But Bob Russell gives us a powerful antidote in this wonderful book. Written from a pastor's heart, *Money: A User's Manual* gives clear, scriptural guidance on how to use your possessions in a way that will make a difference for eternity. Don't miss this important book."

"I have learned to expect special things from Bob Russell, and once again, I am not disappointed. He is blessed with an understandable and relevant way of communicating God's Word. This book is *must* reading."

"The teachings Bob unveils are so relevant and the illustrations so vivid that every reader will think, 'I can do that,' and will be better for it. Even after thirty years of providing stewardship counsel to congregations, by reading this book I've been inspired to help others discover the joy, the freedom, and the victory about which Bob Russell teaches."

MONEY
A USER'S MANUAL

MONEY
A USER'S MANUAL

Bob Russell

with Rusty Russell

MULTNOMAH BOOKS SISTERS, OREGON

MONEY: A USER'S MANUAL
published by Multnomah Books
a part of the Questar publishing family

© 1997 by Bob Russell

International Standard Book Number: 0-57673-037-9

Cover photo by Myron Taplin/Tony Stone Images

Cover design by Kevin Keller

Printed in the United States of America

Scripture quotations are from:
The Holy Bible, New International Version (NIV)
© 1973, 1984 by International Bible Society,
used by permission of Zondervan Publishing House

For information:
QUESTAR PUBLISHERS, INC.
POST OFFICE BOX 1720
SISTERS, OREGON 97759

Library of Congress Cataloging-in-Publication Data:
Russell, Bob, 1943–
    Money: a user's manual/by Bob Russell.
        p. cm.
    Includes bibliographical references.
    ISBN 1-57673-037-9
    1. Finance, Personal. 2. Clergy--Finance, Personal. 3. Finance,
Personal--Religious aspects--Christianity. I. Title.
HG179.R824   1997
332.024--dc21   97-5374
                                                                      CIP
97 98 99 00 01 02 03 04 — 10 9 8 7 6 5 4 3 2 1

In memory of my father,
Charles Russell.
He stored up treasures in heaven.

CONTENTS

INTRODUCTION

I grew up rich and poor.

Financially speaking, we were poor. My parents struggled to provide the material necessities for their six children. My dad worked in the Talon Zipper factory in Meadville, Pennsylvania. He didn't like his job much, and it didn't pay well, but he began working there during the Depression at a time when a person was glad to have any job. He was once promoted to foreman, but unlike me, he didn't like telling people what to do. He asked to return to the line.

I remember a time when I only owned two pairs of socks. I remember eating meat at mealtimes only once or twice a week because we couldn't afford to buy more. About twice a year our parents would splurge and buy us ice cream.

I remember one Christmas when we couldn't afford a Christmas tree and another when I received only one present—a basketball goal. But it was one of my happiest Christmases because that was all I wanted.

Growing up, I often heard, "Sorry, we can't afford that," and learned to accept it without resentment. We weren't poverty-stricken, but money was tight. My parents purchased a small farm, where we raised a garden and milked a few cows. That not only provided us with some vegetables and milk but also created worthwhile chores for us kids. My primary responsibility was to milk the cows every morning. I learned valuable lessons on the farm that still affect the way I view work and money.

Even though we were financially poor, I grew up spiritually wealthy. My parents provided me with the richest spiritual experience imaginable. From the time I was born, we went to church every time the doors were open. Dad was an elder at a small

Christian Church in northwestern Pennsylvania, and he insisted we be in our pew—third from the front on the right side of the aisle—for each service. We never asked, "Are we going to church?" We just asked what time we were leaving.

One Sunday morning we awakened to discover twenty inches of snow had fallen overnight. My younger brother and I, who usually complained about having to go to church so often, were sure this would be the first Sunday ever that we wouldn't have to go. We were wrong.

My parents piled all six children in the car, and we headed for the church fourteen miles away. About a half-mile from home we got stuck in a snowdrift. When the car wouldn't budge, we trudged all the way back home, single file in the car tracks.

My brother and I exchanged knowing glances. We were certain we could now escape to the barn to shoot basketball! Wrong again.

Dad sat us all down in the living room and read the Bible to us. My sister plunked out some choruses on the piano as we sang. Mother went to the kitchen and returned with saltine crackers and grape Kool-Aid, and we took communion together as a family. To this day, that is the most memorable church service I've ever attended.

I grew up spiritually rich.

My mother taught me Bible stories and helped me memorize Scripture from the time I was old enough to talk. Dad set a positive example of a genuine Christian life every day. I never heard my father swear or lie. I never saw him smoke, take a drink, or cheat anyone.

My dad also taught me a lot about the right attitude toward money. He earned it honestly, spent it cautiously, and gave sacrificially. I remember going with him to the bank when he borrowed twenty-five hundred dollars to give to the church to keep it afloat during a precarious time. He then took a second job, working in a sawmill, to pay back the loan.

Though my parents didn't have much, they believed we shouldn't resent those who had more. At times we even felt sorry for them. We couldn't believe that the other children in the neighborhood, who were not so poor, didn't get up on Christmas morning until after eight o'clock. (We started heckling our parents at five in the morning because we were so excited to open our presents.) We concluded that the children next door must have so many things that it was hard for them to get excited about more presents on Christmas Day, and we felt sorry they weren't thrilled about Christmas morning.

Today I still consider myself spiritually rich. Besides my relationship with Jesus Christ, I am blessed with a wonderful wife, two great Christian sons, two pretty and talented daughters-in-law, and a joyous, vivacious grandson. My wife, although she suffered a stroke in 1995, is now healthy, and we have been happily married for more than thirty years. I am privileged to preach in a church that averages ten thousand attendees each Sunday. I am blessed with a supportive, talented staff of associate ministers who get along with each other.

I'm not only rich spiritually, I'm rich financially. A recent article in a financial magazine defined a rich person as someone who earns seven hundred thousand dollars a year or has five million dollars in savings. By that standard I'm not even close, but compared to my past and compared to people living in Third-World countries, I know I am very rich.

I live in a beautiful home more than twice the size of our first house. I have two nice cars, and I am out of debt with the exception of my home mortgage (which will be retired after just 139 more payments!). The church where I have been preaching for the past thirty years has provided a generous salary, and I have enough money that I don't have to worry about my daily needs.

In every stage of life, I have had to learn to manage material things according to God's manual, the Bible. When we were poor,

I was forced to budget strictly and learn how to stay out of debt. Now that we are comparatively rich, I have to deal with a different set of temptations. I heard Gordon MacDonald say that he learned an unguarded strength could become a double weakness. I never thought that greed, hoarding, and indulgence would be temptations I would have to battle. But I've discovered that whether I'm rich or poor, I can return to the principles I learned from my parents and God's Word to overcome the financial temptations and traps that I face.

I believe there is one key to maintaining a spiritual equilibrium when facing the financial hurdles and traps of this world—we must remember that God is the owner of all things and we are temporarily handling his resources. The Bible says, "Now it is required that those who have been given a trust must prove faithful" (1 Corinthians 4:2).

This book addresses the need for Christians to handle material things according to the principles given us by their true Owner. God's Word is a practical guide for handling money, whether we have much or little. Although I've included some practical guides for budgeting and long-term planning, this book is not a detailed financial planner. Its purpose is to encourage you to develop a Christlike attitude toward money. It is a call to remember, "A man's life does not consist in the abundance of his possessions" (Luke 12:15).

Money, A User's Manual is written with the hope that those of us who have been given much will be faithful to the true Owner and will remember, "From everyone who has been given much, much will be demanded; and from the one who has been entrusted with much, much more will be asked" (Luke 12:48).

PART 1

•

BEGINNING WITH
THE RIGHT
PERSPECTIVE

CHAPTER ONE

Money Is *Not* the Root of All Evil

The blessing of the LORD brings wealth,
and he adds no trouble to it.
PROVERBS 10:22

A faithful man will be richly blessed,
but one eager to get rich will not go unpunished.
PROVERBS 28:20

Heavyweight boxer Mike Tyson thinks he's underpaid.

Tyson received thirty million dollars when he knocked out Frank Bruno on March 16, 1996, in the third round. A week later, the *Chicago Tribune* reported that Tyson felt he was worth more money than what he had received. "There's no one who's going to draw like I draw," he said. Yet the seventy-five million dollars he earned in 1996 was more than any athlete in modern history has ever received in one year.[1]

While none of us may find ourselves in Tyson's seventy-five-million-dollar shoes, our perspective on money matters may be just as faulty. Without being conscious of it, we may fall prey to some common misconceptions about who should have money and how much.

MISCONCEPTIONS ABOUT MONEY

Misconception 1: It's Unspiritual to Be Rich

When we hear how much money athletes receive, some of us might be tempted to say, "Nobody should make that much." But there's no passage in the Bible that says, "Thou shalt not make seventy-five million dollars a year."

You might ask, "But doesn't the Bible say, 'Money is the root of all evil'?" No, it doesn't. The Bible says, "For the *love* of money is a root of all kinds of evil" (1 Timothy 6:10, emphasis added). Tyson's problem is not that he made seventy-five million in a year; his problem is that he can't find contentment with what he has.

Those who say that all money is basically evil are misinterpreting the Bible. Many Christians feel guilty for making a lot of money, thinking if they were really spiritual, they would quit their jobs, give all their money to the poor, and live on the streets. And those who are not wealthy may feel contemptuous toward those who are, thinking that if someone is rich, he must be materialistic and not very spiritual.

In reality, the Bible says that everything we have, including our money, is a blessing from God. The apostle Paul told Timothy:

> Command those who are rich in this present world not to be arrogant nor to put their hope in wealth, which is so uncertain, but to put their hope in God, *who richly provides us with everything for our enjoyment.* Command them to do good, to be rich in good deeds, and to be generous and willing to share. (1 Timothy 6:17–18, emphasis added)

Paul didn't say, "Timothy, tell all those rich people to quit their jobs because no one should make that much money." Neither did he say, "Tell them to give all their money to the church and then redistribute it to everyone equally." He wasn't so concerned where their money was as where their hearts were. He wanted the rich people to put their hope in God rather than in riches, to do good deeds and be generous.

Misconception 2: Everyone Should Share Equally

More than one hundred years ago, Karl Marx decided it was unfair for some people to own more than others, so he came up with the philosophy of *communism*. More commonly called *socialism* today, this philosophy teaches that everything should be owned in common; all property should be owned, not by the individual, but by the people as a whole, distributed equally by the government.

The teaching of socialism is so popular today that it has infiltrated many churches. Some people, in fact, think the Bible advocates socialism. They reason, "If we were really spiritual, we would do what the Jerusalem church did and pool all our resources."

I heard a discussion between two well-known preachers about wealthy Christians. One said, "I don't think it is biblically wrong for one person to make more than someone else."

The other quipped, "Yes, but it is wrong for him to keep it!"

Such reasoning sounds fine on the surface; the preacher can even quote Scripture to make his point. After all, isn't that basically what the early Jerusalem church did in Acts 4 when all had "everything in common" and there were no needy persons among them? Yes, but to take that scripture alone and use it as an argument for a socialistic economy is to take it out of context and ignore other scriptures. It was the Jerusalem church, not the government, that encouraged the Christians to pool their possessions, and it was done voluntarily.

Author Rousas J. Rushdoony explains:

> The so-called communism of Acts 2:41–47, also cited by ecclesiastical socialists, was simply a voluntary sharing on the part of some (Acts 5). It was limited to Jerusalem. Because the believers took literally the words of Christ concerning the fall of Jerusalem (Matthew 24:1–28), they liquidated their properties there. The wealthier members placed some or all of these funds at the church's disposal, so that a witness could be made to their friends and relatives before Jerusalem fell.[2]

In Jerusalem, some who had more resources willingly gave them up to help those who did not have enough. Not every church, however, had such a system. Later, under more normal conditions, Paul commanded the church not to give handouts to a person if he refused to work, saying, "If a man will not work, he shall not eat" (2 Thessalonians 3:10). Churches were applauded for different levels of generosity throughout the New Testament, even though none of them appear to have pooled all their resources as the church of Jerusalem did in the beginning.

Misconception 3: Prosperity Is a Sign of God's Favor

I heard an evangelist say, "If you ask God for a new car, make sure to tell him what color you want, because you are sure to get it!" That's a dishonest, manipulative, and hypocritical way to teach people about money. As you might guess, I'm not an advocate of the health-and-wealth gospel. God is not some kind of magical genie who grants wishes, allowing anyone who asks to indulge himself however he wants.

God does not promise us financial riches. Some of the most spiritual people I know are poor. Even Jesus was poor while he was on this earth. Riches have nothing to do with spirituality.

God simply chooses to bless people in different ways, and some he chooses to bless with financial resources. He expects us to be good stewards of what he has given us, whether we are rich or poor. We don't have to feel guilty for making a lot of money if it is made honestly and with a proper perspective. Nor do we need to feel unloved by God if we are as poor as church mice.

JESUS' PHILOSOPHY OF ECONOMICS

So what is the proper biblical perspective regarding money? Perhaps the best place to begin answering that question is Matthew 25, where Jesus told his followers a story that has become known as the parable of the talents. He said that a rich landowner went on a long journey and entrusted three of his servants with some of his wealth. Each was given a sum of "talents," a "talent" in Jesus' day being worth about one thousand dollars. One servant was given five talents (or five thousand dollars), another was given two talents (or two thousand dollars), and the third was given one talent (or one thousand dollars). The owner expected each servant to invest the money wisely and do the best he could with what he had been given.

After a long while, the owner came home and asked for an accounting from each of his three servants. The first servant had used the money wisely, worked hard, invested, and profited, until he had doubled the money. The five talents had become ten. The master said, "Well done, good and faithful servant! You have been faithful with a few things; I will put you in charge of many things. Come and share your master's happiness!" (Matthew 25:21).

The second servant had also worked hard and had doubled his investment. Instead of two talents, he had four. The master gave him the same encouragement: "Well done, good and faithful servant! You have been faithful with a few things; I will put you in charge of many things. Come and share your master's happiness!" (Matthew 25:23).

The third servant, however, did nothing with the money. He was lazy and afraid, and he buried it to make sure he didn't lose it. He said to the master, "Here's your money back."

The master was disgusted. He said to his servant: "You wicked, lazy servant! So you knew that I harvest where I have not sown and gather where I have not scattered seed? Well then, you should have put my money on deposit with the bankers, so that when I returned I would have received it back with interest.

"Take the talent from him and give it to the one who has the ten talents" (Matthew 25:26–28).

Jesus' parable reveals three principles of God's attitude toward money.

Principle 1: God Has Entrusted Various Gifts to Each of Us

The talents were not equally distributed among the servants. One was given five talents, another two, and another one. The socialist would have made sure that the eight talents were distributed equally. He would have given three to the first man, three to the second, and then borrowed an additional talent so he could give three to the third man!

God did not intend for us to be made from the same mold. Nothing that he gives us is given equally. He does not equally distribute abilities, intelligence, likable personalities, or attractiveness. Some people will be more talented; some will be smarter; some will be more attractive or better leaders.

Aren't you glad? How boring this world would be if we all looked, dressed, acted, talked, and walked alike. How boring it would be if we each had the same personality or the same ability to make money. God knew we needed variety in order to be creative and fulfilled in this life. Part of that variety comes in the unequal distribution of wealth, according to our hard work and abilities, but mostly according to his generous blessings.

Principle 2: God Gives Us the Freedom to Develop Those Gifts

In Jesus' parable, the master, who represents God, gives talents to his servants, who represent God's people. The servants are responsible directly to the master for what they have been given. They are free to create a return on their investment, and whatever profit they make is theirs to reinvest. Until the master comes to demand an accounting from each of them, they "own" the money and can do with it as they please.

The Old and New Testament advocate such a relationship between God and man. We have the right to "own" things, but we should acknowledge that "our" things come from God and that we will ultimately give an accounting for these things. In a purely socialistic economy, such ownership doesn't happen. No one owns anything or is responsible for anything. Instead, all things are owned in common or by the government.

In a free society, however, we are able to take the profits from what we sell, because we own it. We can reinvest our earnings to see if we can increase what the Master has given us, because the money is ours to reinvest.

Throughout Scripture, the God-given freedom to own things is apparent. Even the eighth commandment, "You shall not steal" (Exodus 20:15), was given by God to protect us from those who would take by force that which rightfully belongs to us.

In Isaiah 65, when God promised future blessings to his people, those blessings included freedom from captivity and the right to own things again: "They will build houses and dwell in them; they will plant vineyards and eat their fruit. No longer will they build houses and others live in them, or plant and others eat" (Isaiah 65:21–22).

In a similar passage, the Lord promised: "I will give them all the prosperity I have promised them. Once more fields will be bought in this land of which you say, 'It is a desolate waste, without men or animals, for it has been handed over to the Babylonians.' Fields will be bought for silver, and deeds will be signed, sealed and witnessed" (Jeremiah 32:42–44).

If a person has the freedom to own property, then he can sell his property at a price that benefits him, as long as there is a willing buyer. That is called free trade.

The wonderful thing about free trade is that both individuals benefit. I might own a plot of land with lemon trees. You might be great at making lemonade. In a free market, we can trade. I can pick my lemons and give you a full basket in exchange for some lemonade. It may only take a half-basket of lemons to make a pitcher of lemonade, but I can afford to give you twice as many lemons as you need. I am willing to do so because your lemonade is so delicious. You could then make a second pitcher of lemonade to use for yourself or to sell to someone else. I am happy with the trade because I got a wonderful pitcher of lemonade. If I want, I could drink half the pitcher and use the other half to bargain with a baker for a loaf of bread. You're happy because you had enough lemons to make yourself another pitcher of lemonade, which you then traded to a butcher for some hamburger.

Do you see where this leads? In a free-market society, each person is encouraged to be creative, to work hard, and to receive the fruits of his labor. The person who refuses to work hurts himself and his family and will suffer the consequences, motivating him to return to work. In a free society, where individuals own things and don't just share everything in common, each person has the freedom to develop to the fullest the gifts God has given him.

Principle 3: Each of Us Will Give an Accounting before God

The Master will return some day. And each of us will stand before God, as the servants stood before their master in Jesus' parable, to give an account of how we handled the resources we were given on this earth.

In the parable, the one-talent servant received a harsh rebuke from his master. He had been lazy, unwilling to work hard. He had been fearful, unwilling to take risks. As a result, his one talent was still one talent. The master called his servant wicked and lazy. Then he took away the one talent he had given him and banished the servant to the "outer darkness."

Have you ever stood before a judge with your future hanging in the balance, knowing that the judge has the power to incarcerate you, fine you, or release you? I've never been in that circumstance, but I have sat before an IRS agent while he was auditing my books. That was frightening enough for me! How much more sobering to realize that one day every one of us will give an accounting to the God of the universe as to how we have used our "talents."

A Case Study

Let's say I developed a grass that stopped growing when it reached four inches in height. Not only that, my discovery, NuGrass, stayed green and healthy throughout the summer months. If you planted NuGrass in your yard, you would never again need to mow your lawn.

Let's suppose I can produce NuGrass seed for ten dollars a bushel, but I want to sell it to you at one hundred dollars a bushel. That's a 1,000 percent profit! You may balk at my price, but if you buy the NuGrass seed for one hundred dollars, you'll never have to mow your lawn again. It saves you the cost of a mower, gas for the mower, and the time you would spend mowing. What homeowner wouldn't take me up on that offer and consider it a good deal? I could sell you the one-hundred-dollar bushel of seed, and we would both be delighted.

You might say, "But it's not honest to take such an exorbitant profit. Maybe you should sell the seed for twenty dollars a bushel." However, you have to consider the years of research on my part and a fair reward. You also have to consider that I may not be able to sell this seed forever, because eventually everyone will have it for their lawns. Then what will I do? If I have spent my whole life in research, I'll have to start a new project, and I'll need some "seed" money for that next project.

You could still argue that I would be making too much money off my discovery. I've heard Christians refer to billionaires and say, "Nobody should be that rich," without thinking through what they're saying. Who decides what is too rich? Where do you draw the line? What about people in Third-World countries who see Americans as a million times richer than they are?

If I were to tell you that from every one-hundred-dollar bushel I gave sixty dollars to charities, then you might claim my profit wasn't wrong. The legitimacy of the profit is determined by two things: the manner in which it is made (is it honest profit?), and the manner in which it is spent (am I a responsible steward?). When we say, "Nobody should be that rich," we're assuming that the person failed to meet one of those two criteria. Either he didn't make the profit legitimately, or he should have been more generous. But more generous than whom? We don't know how generous he has been.

Let's say the first summer I make a one-million-dollar profit, after taxes, from my NuGrass product. What is appropriate for me to do with that money?

I could give it all away. That would certainly be noble but perhaps not the best stewardship.

I could spend it all on myself. That would be sinful.

I could reinvest it all in the company or elsewhere. That would be frugal.

I could do a combination of the above. That would be wise stewardship.

Let's say I decide to do the following with my profit:

- Give one-half of it ($500,000) to my church and other deserving ministries.
- Save one-fourth ($250,000) to help educate my grand-children.
- Invest half of the remainder ($125,000) in the company to cover advertising and other expenses, to make additional profit, and to have more opportunities for wise stewardship.
- Use the rest ($125,000) for living expenses.

Let's say I continue with that formula and my company continues to do well, earning a one-million-dollar profit every year. After the first year, since my grandchildren's education is now paid, I can afford to give away $750,000 a year. I reinvest $125,000 in the company, and with the remaining $125,000, I can still afford a comfortable lifestyle. I might be able to drive a new car, live in a nice house, and take my family to fancy restaurants occasionally. We might even fly to Hawaii for a vacation. Because all you see is the nice car, the nice house, and the extravagant vacation, you might assume I'm "too rich" and not very generous—yet I'm giving away more than three-fourths of my income!

Before you get any ideas, this entire scenario is hypothetical. I know nothing about grass seed, and I've never made close to that kind of money! But this story does illustrate several key points. In a free society, where individuals own things and don't just share everything in common, each person has the freedom to develop fully the gifts God has given him. Since each person is responsible to God for what he has received, and since God alone can see all, we should not judge someone else's level of generosity simply by what we see on the outside. We should refuse to say, "No one should be that rich," or scoff at someone else's supposed extravagance.

When I stand before God, I want to know I've done everything I can to be a good steward of what God has entrusted to me. I know I'm far from perfect, and I'm thankful the blood of Christ cleanses me from sin so I don't have to fear the "outer darkness." But I want to do my best to be responsible with the gifts he has given me so I can stand before God and receive his promised blessing. I want to hear him say, "Well done, good and faithful servant. Enter into your master's happiness."

As a servant of the Master, I want to know how he would have me handle the "talents" he has entrusted to me. How can I avoid being like the one-talent man? Is there any danger of being overzealous in investing my talents? How does God view my work as a significant part of investing my talents?

That's what we'll look at next.

CHAPTER TWO

Is Work a Curse?

"Whatever you do, work at it with all your heart, as working for the Lord, not for men, since you know that you will receive an inheritance from the Lord as a reward. It is the Lord Christ you are serving."
COLOSSIANS 3:23–24

"I firmly believe that man's finest hour, his greatest fulfillment to all he holds dear, is that moment when he has worked his heart out in a good cause and lies exhausted on the field of battle, victorious."
VINCE LOMBARDI, FORMER HEAD COACH, GREEN BAY PACKERS

If you found out tonight that a distant relative had died and left you ten million dollars, what would you do? Most people would say, "I'd pay off my bills, buy a new car and a condo on the beach, and never work another day for the rest of my life!"

According to the Princeton Management Association, 82 percent of Americans say they hate their jobs. Most people see work as a necessary evil, something they must endure until that blessed, far-off event called retirement.

Christians aren't much different. We usually see our jobs as a secular activity to be tolerated until we can get to church and deal with the things that have eternal significance. In fact, many Christians wrestle with guilt because they believe if they were really dedicated, they would quit their jobs and become full-time Christian workers.

In their book *Your Work Matters to God*, Doug Sherman and William Hendricks articulate what God's Word says about our jobs:

Every day, millions of workers go to work without seeing the slightest connection between what they do all day and what they think God wants done in the world. For example, you may sell insurance, yet you may have no idea whether or not God wants insurance to be sold. Does selling insurance matter to God or not? If not, you are wasting your life.... We think your work matters deeply to God.... It is not something we do apart from God, as the secular world would view it. It is not something beneath God's dignity and concern, as [some Christians view it].... Work is a major part of human life that God takes very seriously. It has intrinsic value. It is inherently worth doing. Through work we serve people, meet our own needs, meet our family's needs, earn money to give to others, and through work we love God.[1]

WORK IS A BLESSING, NOT A CURSE

We usually think of work as God's punishment. We picture an angry God thundering at Adam and Eve, "You have sinned! There is only one fitting punishment for your disobedience. You shall have to work every day of your lives!"

But work isn't a form of punishment, because God himself is a worker. For six days he labored, designing the universe, developing the balance of nature, fashioning the plant and animal kingdoms, and then forming man from the dust of the earth. When he finished his work of creation, he rested for a day and then went back to work. Jesus said, "My Father is always at his work to this very day, and I too am working" (John 5:17).

We forget that God gave work to Adam and Eve *before* they sinned. Genesis 2:15 says, "The LORD God took the man and put him in the Garden of Eden to work it and take care of it." Adam was given work even before he was given a wife! Work was a part of their perfect existence.

It was not work itself that came as a result of sin, but painful and difficult work. After Adam and Eve disobeyed God's command and ate the forbidden fruit, the Lord came to Adam and said, "Cursed is the ground because of you; through painful toil you will eat of it all the days of your life. It will produce thorns and thistles for you, and you will eat the plants of the field. By the sweat of your brow you will eat your food until you return to the ground" (Genesis 3:17–19).

Work may be more difficult and painful because of Adam's curse, but God's original intention for work was for our good—so that we would have a sense of self-worth, our relationships would be enhanced, and our physical needs would be met. Work still meets those needs.

WORK IS ESSENTIAL TO OUR WELL-BEING

I remember the first job I ever had. I worked in a nursery hoeing weeds around the seedlings. It was awful. I hoed for eight hours a day, making eighty cents an hour! I remember thinking there was no way I could last all day long. But I also remember standing at the end of a row and looking back at the clean, cultivated seedlings, thinking to myself, *Good job.*

Whenever I get depressed, I can usually trace the cause to one of two things. Either someone has wounded my ego, or I feel guilty because I haven't worked as hard as I think I should have. Conversely, nothing gets me out of depression faster than putting my hand to a task and accomplishing something.

God created us with an emotional need that can only be met by an honest day's work. Every person, having been made in the image of the Creator, has a God-given desire to imitate him and create. We long to accomplish a task, to do something valuable. When we complete a difficult task, we feel satisfaction and a greater sense of self-respect. Ecclesiastes 3:13 reads, "That everyone may eat and drink, and find satisfaction in all his toil—this is the gift of God." Work is a gift from God, and finding satisfaction in our work is a double blessing.

Such fulfillment comes from any job done well and isn't measured by the money paid for it. Cultivating a garden, remodeling a home, volunteering at church, and many other jobs that don't bring a paycheck sometimes provide much greater fulfillment than income-producing jobs. I've heard mothers say that caring for their young children is the most rewarding job they've ever had, though they get no financial compensation.

My son Phil is a video producer. He loves putting together videos for businesses and ministries to use in promoting their organization or educating their employees. When he is finished splicing videos, superimposing titles, adding musical backgrounds, and condensing the finished product to the right time frame, he feels fulfilled. He will often bring one to our house and say, "Watch this! What do you think?" I seldom see him more fulfilled than in those moments just after he has completed a difficult task.

You might dream of the day you never have to work again, but I see many people who don't have to work become depressed. Someone who retires early or inherits a large amount of money can grow restless and discouraged if he doesn't find some type of meaningful work. He misses the fulfillment that comes from a job well done.

I know a man who made millions in his business, then sold it so he could retire early. Three months later he bought an auto repair shop and began working again. "I have to do something," he said. "I don't need the money, but I need the work."

We have hundreds of older people at our church who volunteer during the week to clean the building, set up for future services, provide security, staff the library, man the gymnasium check-in counters, and prepare the Wednesday-night fellowship meals. They save the church thousands of dollars, and while some of their less-active peers are growing bored and cynical, they are joyful, contented, and fulfilled. Many of them are more fulfilled in their volunteer work than they ever were in their careers.

In his book *Christians in the Marketplace*, Bill Hybels wrote,

> Dignity is available to every person in every worthwhile profession.... The farmer who plows a straight furrow, the accountant whose books balance, the truck driver who backs a forty-foot rig into a narrow loading dock, the teacher who delivers a well-prepared lesson, the carpenter who keeps the building square, the executive who reads the market accurately, the factory worker who labors with speed and accuracy, the secretary who types the pages perfectly, the student who masters a foreign language, the athlete who plays the game aggressively, the mother who tends the children faithfully, the minister who prepares his sermon and preaches it powerfully, all experience dignity as they commit themselves to their labors.[2]

Have you ever become so caught up in an enjoyable task that you lost all track of time? I think heaven will be like that. We usually think of heaven as a place where we will lie around all day, strumming harps. If your job wears you out, that may seem like a good deal for a while, but eventually you would get bored and want to do something meaningful.

An even better existence would be to have a task you enjoy doing, where you cannot fail and never get tired. The Bible describes heaven as a place where we will be given such work by God. Revelation 22:3 says, "No longer will there be any curse. The throne of God and of the Lamb will be in the city, and his servants will serve him." You will be serving God, doing the job for which you were created. It will be so enjoyable that time will fly. You'll never get bored, and you will never fail.

WORK IS A PARTNERSHIP WITH GOD

Some of my fondest memories of childhood are of working with my father, putting up fence posts, weeding the garden, baling hay, and doing other chores around the farm, because working together enhances relationships. God created mankind to have fellowship with him. He planted a garden and put Adam and Eve there to cultivate it. Thus, the first business partnership began.

When we work, we are business partners with God in meeting the needs of the world around us. People need food, clothing, shelter, protection, education, love, and encouragement as well as a saving knowledge of Jesus Christ. God is depending on us to fulfill those needs.

There are 220 different occupations mentioned in the Bible, and they are all partnerships with God. When Moses and the Israelites were preparing to build the tabernacle, Moses said to the Israelites:

"See, the LORD has chosen Bezalel son of Uri, the son of Hur, of the tribe of Judah, and he has filled him with the Spirit of God, with skill, ability and knowledge in all kinds of crafts—to make artistic designs for work in gold, silver and bronze, to cut and set stones, to work in wood and to engage in all kinds of artistic craftsmanship. And he has given both him and Oholiab son of Ahisamach, of the tribe of Dan, the ability to teach others. He has filled them with skill to do all kinds of work as craftsmen, designers, embroiderers in blue, purple and scarlet yarn and fine linen, and weavers—all of them master craftsmen and designers. So Bezalel, Oholiab and every skilled person to whom the LORD has given skill and ability to know how to carry out all the work of constructing the sanctuary are to do the work just as the Lord has commanded." (Exodus 35:30–36:1)

The Lord equipped certain people with the skill, ability, and knowledge to build the tabernacle. And Moses says they were *filled with the Spirit of God.* They were ordained by God just as if they had been called to the priesthood, but they were construction workers, performing their tasks to the best of their abilities. Some of them were ordained to teach others how to do the work. All of them were challenged to do their work "just as the Lord has commanded." They were partners with God in accomplishing God's will.

GOD WILL JUDGE OUR WORK

Paul commanded: "He who has been stealing must steal no longer, but must work, doing something useful with his own hands, that he may have something to share with those in need" (Ephesians 4:28).

In that verse, four criteria are implied by which God evaluates our work.

- God will judge our motives. We are to work so that we might "have something to share with those in need."
- God will judge our effort. Paul said simply, "Work."
- God will judge our integrity. Paul commanded them to "stop stealing."
- God will judge our usefulness. We are to do something "useful" with our hands.

God Will Judge Our Motives

Why do you work? Most people say, "To make money." That's not wrong if their motive for wanting money is pure. If we want to make money so that we can provide for the needs of our family and be generous with what God has given us, then making money is not a wrong motive. If our motivation is simply to get rich or to have nicer things, then we need to purify our motives.

The television program *48 Hours* recently focused on the efforts of three Americans to get rich quick.

The first clip was an exposé of a man's real estate investment scheme. (We'll call him Frank Smith.) His advertisements enticed viewers by making huge promises: "Are you ready to make big money? Frank Smith can help you learn how to buy real estate for no cash and no credit, then resell it for incredible profit. You can attend his first seminar free!" The ads pictured Smith riding in a beautiful convertible with three bikini-clad girls sitting atop the backseat. After showing exotic homes, swimming pools, and fine jewelry, the ads promised it would all be yours "if you just attend Frank Smith Wealth Creation University."

The free seminar, however, was just a teaser to get people to sign up for a two-day seminar, which cost fifteen hundred dollars. That two-day seminar was also just a teaser for a five-day seminar that cost fifteen thousand dollars! The staff of *48 Hours* interviewed scores of people who had attended all three seminars. Of the 130 people who had completed the course, no one claimed to have made much money. It appeared that Smith was making his money, not in real estate, but off those who took his course, wanting to get rich quick.

The second segment related how some people specialize in winning radio call-in prizes. They keep their radios tuned to the stations offering significant prizes and monitor them all day. When a radio announcer says, "The eleventh caller will receive a one-thousand-dollar cash prize," they begin dialing the radio station. Some of them have a battery of three or four phones with speed dials. As soon as the announcement airs, they frantically dial all their phones, hoping to get through. One man showed calluses on his fingers from all his dialing. He claimed to have won more than two hundred thousand dollars' worth of goods from radio stations in the past several years. He apparently didn't bother hunting for a regular job.

The third feature was called "For Love or Money." They interviewed the author of the book *How to Marry a Millionaire*. She admitted she was a gold digger and that she married her husband for his money. "I love men," she said. "They have given me about everything I have." She even offered a course on how to find and attract wealthy men. She schooled her students in what colors they should wear, how they should walk, and how they could recognize wealthy men. She even listed the most likely places to meet and marry a six-million-dollar man!

Why do people go to such lengths to get money without working for it? Paul told Timothy, "The love of money is a root of all kinds of evil. Some people, eager for money, have wandered from the faith and pierced themselves with many griefs" (1 Timothy 6:10).

We are not to work just for more money or ego gratification. We are to work so that we might "have something to share with those in need" (Ephesians 4:28). God is not nearly as concerned with how much money we make as he is with our motives for making it, and what we do with it after we earn it.

God Will Judge Our Efforts

At the 1996 Summer Olympics in Atlanta, Michael Johnson won the gold medal in the 200-meter dash and the 400-meter dash, breaking the world record in the 200-meter. After the 200-meter race, Johnson was asked, "Is that the fastest a human being can possibly go?"

"Oh, no," he answered. "I think I could run it faster. I made a small mistake on my fourth step that I would like to correct before the next competition."

We all have a God-given desire, not just to work, but to excel and improve. Thorvaldsen, the famous sculptor, was once asked which of his works he considered to be the greatest. "My next one," he replied.

The concertmaster of the Louisville orchestra, Michael Davis, is a member of our church. He told me he still practices the violin four or five hours a day. Since he has already reached the pinnacle of success, why does he continue to practice so much? He wants to get better. He is not in competition with everyone else. He wants to be the best violinist he can be, and he knows he hasn't achieved that yet.

Three out of four Sundays I go home feeling a little down because I believe I could have done better on my sermon. In fact, when I become satisfied and complacent, God seems to bring someone into my path to drive me forward again. I once commented to my wife as we were walking to the car after church that I felt really good about my sermon. I delivered it just as I intended at each of the four services. Later, a young man who used to be one of our interns approached me during our lunch at a local restaurant. "Bob," he said, "I wish I could have heard you in an earlier service. You seemed tired and a little below par today." His words were humbling, but they also motivated me not to be complacent. I know I can always do better.

Paul wrote, "Brothers, I do not consider myself yet to have taken hold of it. But one thing I do: Forgetting what is behind and straining toward what is ahead, I press on toward the goal to win the prize for which God has called me heavenward in Christ Jesus" (Philippians 3:13–14).

Paul didn't say, "I've been on two missionary journeys, and I've been nearly killed on both of them. I've done my duty, and it's time to retire before I get really hurt." He envisioned going to Rome, then to Spain, and being able to preach all over the world.

In another passage, the apostle commanded, "Whatever you do, work at it with all your heart, as working for the Lord, not for men, since you know that you will receive an inheritance from the Lord as a reward. It is the Lord Christ you are serving" (Colossians 3:23–24).

While Christians should maintain a healthy balance between work and rest, we should not be lazy. The Book of Proverbs is filled with condemnation for the lazy or slothful person. According to Proverbs, the lazy person will...

- be poor (Proverbs 10:4)
- irritate those around him (Proverbs 10:26)
- serve someone else (Proverbs 12:24)
- never be satisfied (Proverbs 13:4)
- have difficult obstacles to overcome (Proverbs 15:19)
- be paranoid of unrealistic danger (Proverbs 22:13)

When we are lazy, we bring disgrace to ourselves and are a poor reflection of the character of God. When we work hard, we honor God.

God Will Judge Our Integrity

When I was a boy, we used to pick elderberries and sell them so we could have enough money to go to the state fair. Then one day someone said to us, "Do you know what they do with those elderberries? They make elderberry wine and people get drunk off of it!" We were devastated until my dad assured us that *our* elderberries were used to make elderberry *jam*, not wine.

The money we make should come from legitimate, honest work, but it's not always easy to tell whether a job benefits an immoral cause. A high school classmate of mine began selling encyclopedias while he was in college to pay for his education. He was trained by the company to knock on someone's door and say to the person who answered, "Congratulations! Your family has been selected as one of several families in the area to receive a free set of encyclopedias!"

He would ask to be invited into the home so he could show them the product and have them fill out the proper forms. After spreading out the encyclopedias and showing the family what a great prize they had won, he would say, "Now, of course, we will expect you to do one thing as our representatives in the neighborhood, and that is to purchase the one-volume update printed each year, at a cost of just fifty dollars a year." By that time the family was usually so excited about the encyclopedias, they didn't realize they were agreeing to pay for the entire set of encyclopedias over several years' time.

If a family would admit they couldn't afford to buy the new volumes, he was trained to fake indignation and say, "I can't believe it! We're giving you a complete set of encyclopedias free, and you don't care enough to buy one book a year? What's wrong with you people! I've wasted this entire presentation." In a huff, he would begin folding up his promotional material. The family would often cave in to the pressure and agree to buy the annual volume.

Then one day, in the middle of a presentation, my friend could tell that the beautiful family he was trying to manipulate couldn't really afford the encyclopedias and didn't really need them. They were nonetheless excited about the prize they thought they had won. He liked them so much that his conscience started to bother him.

He stopped in the middle of his presentation, looked up at them, and said, "Folks, I can't do this to you. This is not honest. I'm trying to sell you this set of encyclopedias at an outrageous price."

He folded up the charts and began answering all of their questions with the truth about the scam. The family loved him for his honesty. They asked him to stay for a while and visit, and he began developing a relationship with them that has lasted a lifetime.

My friend found another way to work his way through college. Today he is a respected educator and a leader in his church.

It's not always easy to determine whether our work is benefiting an immoral cause or manipulating someone, so each of us should examine his work and ask God for wisdom. If you conclude that you are involved in a task that is contrary to God's will, look for a way out. Pray that God will provide an open door for you to create positive change in your workplace so that the business becomes ethical, or that God will lead you to a new job.

In most instances, our work honors God. He has given us specific abilities and desires to motivate us to work so that the needs of his world might be met. He expects us to work hard, to be honest, and to be good stewards of that which he allows us to earn.

God Will Judge Our Usefulness

God will also judge us by how our job contributes to the overall benefit of others. We make a mistake when we leave the impression that being an ordained minister is a more spiritual occupation or "calling" than another job. I heard a man say, "I was working as an engineer, designing bridges. Then one day I realized, God is going to burn up all these bridges some day. What significance is there in designing and building bridges? I want to be involved in something that lasts for eternity. That's why I quit designing bridges, and now I'm a missionary in God's service." He left the impression that if you're a design engineer, you're a second-rate Christian, and that if you're really dedicated, you would quit your job and become involved in eternal matters.

But God doesn't have a two-tiered scale of service. Author Myron Rush said, "Satan's immaculate deception is that we send some people into full-time work and others are spectator Christians."

I love how one Christian woman responded when asked what she did for a living. She said, "I am a missionary for Jesus Christ, cleverly disguised as a checkout clerk at Kroger." We are *all* called to be ministers, no matter what our jobs are. The apostle John wrote, "To him who loves us and has freed us from our sins by his blood, and has made us to be a kingdom and priests to serve his

God and Father—to him be glory and power for ever and ever! Amen" (Revelation 1:5–6).

It's true that God calls some of us into paid ministries, like teaching and preaching and evangelism and mission work, which are worthy of honor and are tremendous blessings. God also equips people to design bridges so the evangelist doesn't fall into the river and kill himself on the way to church. The engineer who designs bridges to the glory of God is just as important in God's plan as the minister who preaches sermons.

Are you a nurse? Then you are a partner with God in helping to restore his people to health or to alleviate their discomfort.

Are you a school teacher? Then you are a partner with God in developing his children so that they grow intellectually.

Are you an artist, an entertainer, or a musician? Then you are a partner with God in encouraging people and giving them a glimpse of the creative, joyful spirit of the Lord.

If you are a youth minister, a psychologist, a social worker, a doctor, or a mother, you may easily see how your occupation helps people and serves God. If you are a cashier, a data processor, or an IRS agent, you may wonder how your work fits into God's plan. But even if the answer is not obvious, consider all the jobs and services needed to provide for people's needs and to enhance our world. Truly, every legitimate occupation is a partnership with God.

William Hendricks tells a tale of a man who owned a company that made pallets, the platforms used to enable forklifts to move stacks of goods. You might say, "How can that man's pallets possibly fit into the work of God in the world?" But Hendricks explained that those pallets were an indispensable part of the trucking industry—an industry that delivers red grapefruit from the Rio Grande Valley, boxes of cereal from Battle Creek, Michigan, and milk from the local dairy to the supermarket near our homes. All of those products come together at the breakfast table.

Before we eat, we thank God for the food. Why? Because he brought to our table something we needed. But God has used a complex system of workers to give us that food. He used farmers to plant and cultivate the citrus trees and wheat and to raise the dairy cows. He used scientists to check the food for purity, bankers to arrange financing, engineers and machinists to assemble the farm equipment, and salesmen and dealers to provide the equipment. He used trucks and their drivers to haul the food. What about the truck-stop operators along the way who provided diesel fuel and coffee, the construction workers who laid the pavement, and the supermarket employees who scanned the food at the cash registers? They are important too. God has used all of these people along the way to meet your family's needs.

Once you grasp that concept about your own job, it can revolutionize your attitude toward work. You are performing a task not just to draw a paycheck or to please your employer, but to serve God and your fellow man.

One Christian explained why he invests in restaurants and fast-food stores. He said, "I like to take a raw piece of land and make it productive. The store or restaurant I put up sells food and other items that people need. And it provides an income for the employees I hire. It also gives me a good return on my investment." All of those benefits can bring honor and glory to God.

A few years ago, while I was traveling along an interstate highway, I saw a large sign over a business that read, "H&S Farm Equipment Company. To God Be the Glory." How inspiring! Someone in that organization had discovered that you go to work for the same reason you go to church—to worship and serve Christ.

CHAPTER THREE

THE SUCCESS TRAP

People who want to get rich fall into temptation and a trap and into many foolish and harmful desires that plunge men into ruin and destruction.

1 TIMOTHY 6:9

He who dies with the most toys wins.

A POPULAR BUMPER STICKER

Charles Barkley, a star player in the National Basketball Association, said his mother was upset with him because he had voted for George Bush in the 1992 presidential election. "Charles," she said, "George Bush is the rich people's president!"

"Mom," he answered, "we *are* the rich people!"

Most of us classify a rich person as anyone making twice what we make. You may not make the multimillion-dollar salary that Charles Barkley makes, but if you compared yourself with the rest of the world, you would probably consider yourself very wealthy.

If you have ever visited a Third-World country, you have seen true poverty. Even if you live on welfare in America, you are wealthier than 95 percent of the people living in East Africa, India, or Mexico. If you can afford to buy this book, millions of people in the world would consider you wealthy!

In 1 Timothy 6, when Paul refers to "those who are rich in this present world," we should listen because he is talking about us. He writes, "Command those who are rich in this present world not to be arrogant nor to put their hope in wealth, which is so uncertain, but to put their hope in God, who richly provides us with everything for our enjoyment. Command them to do good, to be rich in good deeds, and to be generous and willing to share. In this way they will lay up treasure for themselves as a firm foundation for the coming age, so that they may take hold of the life that is truly life" (1 Timothy 6:17–19).

Why is financial success a potential trap? Notice that Paul began by saying, "Command those who are rich...not to be *arrogant*." Financial success brings with it a temptation to become proud of ourselves, and in that pride we become vulnerable to three traps.

A FEELING OF SUPERIORITY

Jesus said, "A man's life does not consist in the abundance of his possessions" (Luke 12:15). Deep down we know that's true, and we give verbal consent, telling our kids, "There are more important things than money." In reality, we frequently measure people by their financial status.

"He may not look like much," we say, "but he's worth two million dollars." Or, "She's a 51 percent shareholder in the company...and she drives a Jaguar." I even hear parents encouraging their children to date someone from a wealthy family. "Money isn't everything," they'll say, "but it sure doesn't hurt."

When your neighbors have more than you, it's tempting to feel inferior. In the same way, when you have more than your neighbors, you may be tempted to feel superior. If you buy a new car, for a few days you may look down your nose at all the people driving old clunkers. If you move into a house on the nice side of town, you may be tempted to feel better than those living in the old neighborhood. If you buy your clothes at Talbots or Saks, you may feel more important than someone shopping at Wal-Mart.

While that attitude is obvious in American society, it isn't new to our culture. James wrote in James 2:1–6:

My brothers, as believers in our glorious Lord Jesus Christ, don't show favoritism. Suppose a man comes into your meeting wearing a gold ring and fine clothes, and a poor man in shabby clothes also comes in. If you show special attention to the man wearing fine clothes and say, "Here's a good seat for you," but say to the poor man, "You stand there" or "Sit on the floor by my feet," have you not discriminated among yourselves and become judges with evil thoughts?

Listen, my dear brothers: Has not God chosen those who are poor in the eyes of the world to be rich in faith and to inherit the kingdom he promised those who love him? But you have insulted the poor.

The problem goes deeper than just attitudes; it affects our decisions. In 1995, *Fortune* magazine carried an article entitled "The Trophy Wife Is Back with Brains." The author wrote, "Powerful men are beginning to demand trophy wives. The more money men make, the argument goes, the more self-assured they become, and the easier it is for them to think, 'I deserve a queen.' Enter the second wife; a decade or two younger than her husband, sometimes several inches taller, beautiful and very often accomplished."

"The culture of self-indulgence has just crept up to the CEO level," says Boston psychologist Harry Levinson, a longtime counselor to top-management people. "Indulgence is an issue for people who have worked very hard to get where they are. They feel they've earned it, they're entitled to it."[1]

What convoluted thinking! "Now that I have more money," the argument goes, "I am more important. And since *I've* earned it, I deserve better than what I had—no matter how it affects my wife, my children, or my relationship with God."

What would possess us to think we're more important than someone else just because we have more money? Our brains and our leadership ability have little to do with our financial success.

We were blessed to be born during the right technological era, to go to the right school to get a good education, to be in the right place at the right time. We're like the substitute player for the Chicago Bulls who was asked what was his greatest moment in his basketball career. "The night that Michael Jordan and I combined to score seventy points in a basketball game," he said. "MJ had sixty-eight, and I had two!" What we have—including our abilities and circumstances—came from God, and we have no reason to boast except in his glory.

A FALSE SENSE OF SELF-SUFFICIENCY

A rich person can also be tempted to think, *I don't need those old friends, I don't need the church, and I don't need God now that I can buy my way wherever I want to go and do whatever I want to do.*

A preacher I know told of a friend who had lived frugally and saved sacrificially to put money into an account that he named his good-bye-to-you account (to put it in polite language). When he finally reached his goal of having more than his annual salary in the account, he took his bank statement and showed it to his boss. He wasn't quitting his job; he was just explaining that if ever the boss didn't treat him right or things went wrong in the company, he wasn't dependent upon his job. He had saved enough that he could say, "Good-bye to you," if he had to.

We don't like anyone controlling us. We value our independence, and money can make us feel as if we have achieved that independence. We can afford to go where we want to go, to be our own boss if we want. It's not wrong to desire financial independence, but the danger of wealth is that we can become so proud that we believe we don't need anyone anymore—not our spouse, not our boss, not our friends...not even God.

Oswald Sanders, the author of *Spiritual Manpower*, defines pride as "the sin of making self God." Someone else referred to ego as an acrostic meaning "Edging God Out." Psalm 10:4 reads, "In his pride the wicked does not seek him; in all his thoughts there is no room for God."

I heard a speaker describe it this way: "We treat God like we treat a policeman. When we're driving sixty-five miles per hour in a forty-five-miles-per-hour zone, we don't want to see a policeman. But when someone is breaking into our house in the middle of the night, we hope a policeman is close by."

When we're making a lot of money and things are going great, we can feel like we're driving sixty-five in a forty-five-mile-per-hour zone. We don't need God, and we don't want to see him. But such pride always catches up to us.

Within just a few months of the Dallas Cowboys winning the 1996 Super Bowl, their star wide receiver, Michael Irvin, was arrested. The press reported that he and a friend were found in a hotel room with drugs and two dancers from a Dallas nightclub. What an embarrassment to Irvin and his family. What a scar on his reputation and career. He pled guilty to a lesser charge, was paroled, and then was suspended for five games by the National Football League officials. Irvin apologized to his teammates for taking the focus off the Super Bowl win and tarnishing the accomplishment. "My teammates deserve better," he said.

How can someone do something that foolish? Pride. The more money a person makes, the greater the temptation to think he can do whatever he wants and get away with it. But as the Bible promises, "When pride comes, then comes disgrace" (Proverbs 11:2).

Three of the four gospels record for us an encounter between a rich young ruler and Jesus. The young man asked Jesus, "Good teacher, what good thing must I do to get eternal life?"

Jesus began listing the commandments. "Do not murder, do not commit adultery, do not steal, do not give false testimony, honor your father and mother, and love your neighbor as yourself." In other words, live a perfect life and earn your way into heaven.

The young man answered without hesitating, "I've kept all those commandments since I was a little boy." Then, perhaps with a smirk on his face, he asked, "What do I still lack?" (Translate that: "Sounds pretty easy to me, Jesus. Is that it?")

Jesus said, "If you want to be perfect, there is one thing you still lack. Go, sell all your possessions and give to the poor, and you will have treasure in heaven. Then come, follow me."

The man went away sad, because he had great wealth. Jesus turned to the crowd and gave this warning: "How hard it is for the rich to enter the kingdom of God! Indeed, it is easier for a camel to go through the eye of a needle than for a rich man to enter the kingdom of God."

As William Boice, the minister of the First Christian Church in Phoenix, has said, "If the young ruler was rich, what am I?" He never owned a car, a television, a VCR, a telephone, a computer, air conditioning, a washer or dryer, a microwave, or dozens of other things we take for granted.

After the encounter, the disciples asked, "Who, then, can be saved?"

Jesus said, "With man this is impossible, but with God all things are possible." (See Matthew 19:16–24, Mark 10:17–25, Luke 18:18–25.)

If God wanted to, he could get a camel through a needle's eye. But the camel would have to become very small! So it is with us if we want to enter the kingdom of God. We cannot be perfect. It is impossible. We are dependent upon God to save us. But he will require us first to give up our pride and become very small. James said, "God opposes the proud but gives grace to the humble" (James 4:6). Or in common language, "God does not save a strutter."

A DESIRE FOR MORE

John D. Rockefeller was once asked, "How much money does it take to satisfy a man?"

He answered, "Just a little more."

Financial success never satisfies our desire for more. In fact, the temptation often intensifies. The more we have, the more we want, and the more difficult it is for us to humble ourselves before God and acknowledge our dependence on him.

Paul Azinger is a professional golfer who has reached the pinnacle of success, winning several tournaments, including the 1991 PGA Championship. He has a wonderful Christian testimony and has had many opportunities to share it, especially after overcoming a bout with cancer shortly after his 1991 victory.

But Azinger feels he has not fully recovered his golf stroke since his cancer, and it has frustrated him not to play as well as he knows he can. In 1996, during the British Open, he got so angry after missing a putt that he broke his club over his knee, leaving him nine holes to play without his putter.

The following week, the PGA tour event was in Boston, Massachusetts. I happened to be in Boston that week because Ted Schulz, another tour professional, is a member of our church, and I had gone to watch him play.

Ted invited me to go with him to the Bible study they have for pro golfers each Wednesday night. That week only about twelve golfers and some of their family members came to the study. Azinger walked into the room when it was time to start and said, "Larry Moody [who usually directs the Bible study] can't come tonight because his dad is having emergency surgery. I'm not sure what we're going to do."

Somebody pointed to me and said, "I move that the preacher here be in charge." As I started scrambling in my mind for what to say, Azinger responded, "That's fine, but I want to say something first," and then he began pouring out his heart to the guys. "As you all know," he said, "I broke my putter last week in the British Open, and I'm really embarrassed. I feel like I need to apologize to you guys. I know the fruit of the Spirit is self-control, and I really blew it. That story with the picture of me breaking my putter was all over the newspapers in Great Britain and America. One tabloid in Britain said, 'Azinger is supposed to be a Christian, and he lost his temper.'"

Azinger went on to say that he was so humiliated and embarrassed and his self-esteem was so low he didn't even want to show his face in public. "I'm supposed to give my testimony at the PGA Championship in Louisville, Kentucky, in a couple of weeks, and I don't even want to go.

"I realize my problem is pride. My ego is out of control. I'm frustrated because my golf game isn't measuring up. I want to share some Proverbs about pride." After reading several verses from Proverbs, he said, "I know I've got to deal with my pride."

Then Azinger began an impromptu testimony about his golfing career. "When I started playing competitive golf," he said, "my hometown paper asked, 'Is Azinger good enough to make it on the tour?' When I made the tour, they asked, 'Is Azinger good enough to win?' After I won my first tournament, they said, 'Can he sustain it?'

"Then when I was the [PGA] Golfer of the Year, my thrill lasted two days—until I picked up a magazine and read an article that said, 'Is Paul Azinger the best player never to have won a *major* [tournament]?' It's never enough.

"It's like when you get a new car. For a few days it's the greatest and you take special care of it. Then six weeks later it doesn't mean that much. It doesn't satisfy. All my successes on tour haven't really satisfied me. Right now, I'm low. God is humbling me."

One of the golfers said, "Zinger, what are you going to do?"

"I've already gone to my knees and confessed to God and asked his forgiveness," he responded. "I'm asking you to help me too."

Then he turned to me and said, "What do you have to say about that, preacher?"

"Well, a couple of things," I began. (By then I'd had time to think of something!) "First, I think you're right. The problem is pride. Anyone who is a competitor has to deal with it. I have to deal with it in the ministry. I heard someone call it 'the encore mentality.' The next sermon has to be better than the last, no matter how good it was.

"I think the core problem is that we're getting our self-worth from other people and not from God. The Bible says some of the Pharisees believed in Jesus, but they would not confess him publicly because they loved the praise of men more than the praise of God. That's our problem. When we seek praise from men, we're always disappointed, because it's never enough; there has to be something more. We have to come to the point where we say, 'Lord, the praise of people doesn't matter; what matters is that I want to hear you say, "Well done, good and faithful servant."'

"Second, God often takes our greatest failures and uses them for his glory. When we're weak, he becomes strong. The Bible says, 'All things work for good for those who love God.' God can even take our loss of temper and use it for his glory. Charles Colson says that he was proud of his degrees and his office as special counsel to President Nixon, but God didn't use any of that. God took his biggest failure—his humiliation in Watergate and his prison term—and that's what he used. Colson started a dynamic prison ministry as a result.

"Paul, maybe you're going to have more opportunities to witness for Christ as a result of losing your temper than you would have had if you'd won the tournament. Reporters are going to ask you about losing your temper, and you're going to have the opportunity to say, 'I'm a Christian, and I sinned, and I'm embarrassed. But a Christian isn't perfect; he's forgiven.' They'll have to listen because they asked the question. I suspect God has you right now, in your present state, where he wants you, and you may be on the verge of your greatest witness for him."

I ended by saying, "Paul, I'm going to be in the audience at that breakfast in Louisville, and I want you to be there."

The other golfers in the room began confirming what I had said and encouraging Azinger. You could just feel his spirits pick up. He said, "I feel so much better! Thanks for letting me share with you tonight." And we closed in prayer.

It was a special night.

A few weeks later Azinger came to the breakfast in our town and gave a wonderful testimony in front of more than two thousand people. And several responded with decisions for Christ. Paul Azinger is a successful competitor and a wealthy man by the world's standards, but his attitude—asking forgiveness, trusting the Lord for his goodness, acknowledging that God granted him his gift to play golf—is an attitude that God honors and that brings Azinger true success. One word describes that attitude: humility.

Proverbs 29:23 says, "A man's pride brings him low, but a man of lowly spirit gains honor." The lives of Charles Colson and Paul Azinger testify to that truth.

THE SECRET IS HUMILITY

In the Chapel of the Nativity in Bethlehem, the entrance is so low that everyone has to stoop to get in. But if you stand back from the doorway, you can see the outline of an old door that was much larger. It is said that in the Middle Ages, the knights would come to the chapel seeking the priest's blessing before they went on their crusades. Often a knight would proudly ride right through the door and expect to receive a blessing without even dismounting from his horse. The priests finally blocked up the old doorway and made the entrance so small that no one could come seeking God's blessing without getting off his horse and bowing low when he came into the presence of God.

God opposes the proud but gives grace to the humble. The

secret to avoiding the traps of success is to dismount from our high horse and make ourselves small, coming humbly before God and asking for his blessing.

> Turn your eyes upon Jesus,
> Look full in his wonderful face,
> And the things of earth will grow strangely dim
> In the light of his glory and grace.[2]

CHAPTER FOUR

The Comparison Trap

A heart at peace gives life to the body, but envy rots the bones.
PROVERBS 14:30

It's hard to save money when your neighbor keeps buying things you can't afford!
ANONYMOUS

One of Aesop's fables tells of a man who could have anything he desired. The catch was that his neighbor would always get twice as much as he. The man wished for a new home. It was beautiful, but his neighbor's was twice as big. Then he wished for a new horse. He loved his new horse, but it disturbed him that his neighbor now had two wonderful horses. He wished for a new tunic, and instantly it was his. But he had trouble enjoying it because his neighbor's new tunic was twice as nice. The man was eaten up with envy. The fable ends with the man wishing, "I would like to be blind in one eye."

Why do we always envy the grass on the other side of the fence? Our friends seem to be happier, more attractive, richer, and younger looking than we are. Their cars are cleaner, their yards nicer, their kids better behaved, and their lives more exciting.

We can visit a friend's house and come away feeling so discontented. "How can he do it?" we wonder. "His salary is the same as mine. Did you see that beautiful entryway, the three-car garage, that immaculate yard? Their furniture goes back to Louis XIV. Ours goes back to Sears on the fifteenth!"

Many of our financial problems are not rooted in bad accounting techniques. All too often we have financial problems because we fall into the comparison trap. We will spend money we never intended to spend on boats, exercise equipment, cars, clothes, furniture, and vacations, just to "keep up with the Joneses."

Staying out of the comparison trap is essential for achieving financial freedom. It's much easier to spend our money wisely and to honor God if we are not constantly comparing ourselves to others and envying what they have.

So what causes us to fall into the comparison trap? Usually one of three things: low self-esteem, a competitive nature, or a socialistic philosophy toward money.

LOW SELF-ESTEEM

The most common cause of envy is a feeling of inadequacy. If we struggle with low self-esteem, it's tempting to compare ourselves to others who have nicer things and feel inferior to them.

We think our rich friends must consider themselves better than us, and we reason, *Maybe they're right. Maybe I am inferior.* If the truth were known, they probably don't feel that way at all, but we begin wishing things were distributed more evenly. One woman who had difficulty losing weight confessed to being envious of others' appearance. She finally prayed, "Lord, if I can't lose weight, at least make my friends look fat!"

A preacher's self-worth is often based not on how much money he makes but on how many people attend his church. I watched one of President Clinton's State of the Union speeches on television a couple of years ago. At the end of the speech, he introduced several citizens seated with his wife in the audience whom he said exemplified the American spirit. Among those sitting with the first lady were John Cherry and his wife, Diane, pastors of the AME Zion Church in Temple Hills, Maryland. President Clinton explained that the couple had begun a church in their home in the Washington, D.C., area, which by then had reached seventeen thousand members, and that they were adding about two hundred new members a month.

What do you think my first reaction was? *That's wonderful! That's twice as fast as we're growing! Good for them!* If you believe that, you don't know me very well. My first thought was, *Well, seventeen thousand members, but how many actually attend?* The president went on to say that the church was one of the three largest in the nation. I thought, *We're in the top ten, and no one has invited me to the White House!*

Our self-worth can be attacked through our work, our status in the community, or our net worth, but when we allow ourselves to focus on what we don't have compared to others, we step into the comparison trap.

COMPETITIVE NATURE

The following "greed game" illustrates another reason we fall into the comparison trap: our desire to get our fair share.

> Psychologist Julian Edney used to organize a greed game for groups of college students. He'd place ten metal nuts in a bowl and make clear the goal was for each person to get as many as possible because they represented extra credit. Then he would promise that every ten seconds he'd double the number of nuts left in the bowl. Theoretically, the game could go on forever and everyone could reap limitless rewards—if people cooperated. But sixty-five percent of the groups didn't make it past Round One, and most of the rest didn't get past more than a few rounds as mild-mannered students became Hulk-a-maniacs, clawing to get all the nuts. Edney's conclusion: Greed trumps trust.[1]

We are a competitive people. Our drive to have more than those around us can be very strong, causing us to compete not just for material things but for status and prestige too.

A story is told about a demon who comes to Satan, distraught over his inability to lure a godly monk into temptation. "You've been too hard on the monk," Satan says. "Send him a message that his brother has just been made Bishop of Antioch."

Our adversary, Satan, will dangle before us the successes of others in an effort to entice us into the comparison trap. He would love nothing more than for us to feel sorry for ourselves and dwell on how well life has treated others.

While a competitive spirit can be a positive trait, a person who has a type-A personality and is driven to succeed will likely struggle with envy. Kathryn Jenson said, "Life is like being on a dog team. Unless you're the lead dog, all the scenery looks about the same." If so, most people are doomed to a miserable life.

Leonard Bernstein, the famous symphony conductor, was asked what instrument was the most difficult to play. "Second fiddle," he responded. There will always be someone who is more talented, better looking, smarter, or more successful in his business. If we can't be happy without being the first chair in the orchestra or the lead dog on the dog team, then envy is going to eat at our souls for the rest of our lives.

SOCIALISTIC PHILOSOPHY

A third factor that may cause us to fall into the comparison trap is a socialistic perspective. It's common for those who believe in socialism—the philosophy that all things should be owned by the government and distributed equally among the people—to look down their noses at anyone who has benefited from a free market, or capitalism. They rationalize that someone who is rich is naturally evil and greedy, otherwise he would never allow himself to maintain a higher living standard than others.

If you find yourself assuming a wealthy person cannot be very spiritual or he would give up some of his riches, Satan has entrapped you. Not only have you broken Christ's command not to judge others (Matthew 7:1), you have also broken the command against envy, because you have viewed yourself or the poor as disadvantaged and of less worth than the person who is rich.

Christ doesn't judge in that way. Each of us is judged individually, not in comparison to others, but in comparison to the standard of generosity God has given to us. Jesus said, "From everyone who has been given much, much will be demanded; and from the one who has been entrusted with much, much more will be asked" (Luke 12:48). The more generous God is to you, the more generous he requires you to be toward others. Under this system, it is God who must do the judging, not us.

Christian financial counselor Larry Burkett tells of a man who said, "I own a Mercedes and a home that's probably worth two hundred thousand dollars, but my income is sufficient to buy both of them just as easily as somebody else would buy a Chevrolet and a fifty-thousand-dollar home. Are these indulgences because of their cost, even though they hold their value better than lesser-priced items?"

When we judge a rich person as selfish or conceited, the judgment is usually based on our feelings of envy rather than on a true knowledge of the other person.

THE POWER OF ENVY

One of the biggest problems with comparison and envy may be that we don't treat them as serious problems. They probably don't make most people's short list of "serious sins," but they can have devastating consequences.

Perhaps the most powerful example of envy and its consequences in the Bible is found in 1 Kings 21, in the story of Ahab and Jezebel. Ahab was a proud king of Israel, and Jezebel was his wicked queen. Although they were powerful and rich, Ahab was envious of an attractive vineyard that was adjacent to the palace grounds. Visitors probably complimented Ahab on his well-manicured vineyard and asked if they could stroll through it, but Ahab had to admit that he didn't own the property and it was off-limits. He couldn't stand it.

Ahab offered to buy the vineyard, but Naboth, the owner, didn't want to sell. In fact, Old Testament regulations prohibited Naboth from selling his property to anyone other than a family member. The regulation was the key to maintaining a fair, free-market economy for generations. The Old Testament law also forbade the government from confiscating property, so Ahab was denied his wish. But Ahab couldn't stand being denied anything.

Envy is no respecter of persons. You can be poor and envious of those who are rich, or you can be rich and envious of some minor property you can't have. Envy can drive any of us into the comparison trap, but as we see with Ahab and Jezebel, it exacts a high price.

ENVY DISSOLVES HAPPINESS

After being denied the property, Ahab "went home, sullen and angry because Naboth the Jezreelite had said, 'I will not give you the inheritance of my fathers.' He lay on his bed sulking and refused to eat" (1 Kings 21:4).

Ahab was the king—the wealthiest, most powerful man in the land. Instead of being content with what he had, he focused on what he didn't have and was miserable. He pouted like a child. He went on a hunger strike in protest.

The renaissance artist Giotto attempted to paint envy as a demonic character. He painted Envy with long ears so he could hear every bit of news of another's success. Then he gave Envy the tongue of a serpent that he might poison the reputation of the one being envied, but the tongue coils back and stings the eyes of the figure itself. Giotto captured Envy as being not only blind, but self-destructive.

Envy's power to destroy its possessor is seen not only in Ahab, but in our affluent American society. Marty Seligman, a professor of psychology at the University of Pennsylvania, conducted a study of depression in America. The study showed there has been a sharp increase in depression since World War II. People born after 1945 are ten times more likely to suffer depression than people born fifty years earlier. That's strange, since today we have so many more possessions and life is more comfortable. Seligman said that, on the whole, you do not find much depression as we know it (suicide, hopelessness, giving up, low self-esteem, passivity,) in non-Westernized cultures before they are modernized. Some primitive and less Westernized cultures may not show any depression. A study in 1984 of a primitive tribe in New Guinea found little evidence of despair at all. Another pre-industrialized society—the Amish of Lancaster County, Pennsylvania—showed depression occurring at roughly one-fifth to one-tenth the rate it occurred among the people of Baltimore.

In an attempt to explain why discontentment is so much more common today, Seligman acknowledged that people today are caught up in an attitude of almost complete self-centeredness. All that matters is how I feel, how I look, and what I'm worth. He said there is an erosion of commitment to the nation, which causes a rise in individuals turning inward to look for satisfaction within their own lives. Our children ask what the world owes them, whereas our parents asked what they owed the world.

This waning patriotism coincides with a breakdown of the family, which all took place against the backdrop of a culture with little belief in God. Seligman asked, "Where can we now turn for identity, satisfaction, and hope? To a very small and frail unit indeed—the self. Surely the one necessary condition for meaning is the attachment to something larger than you."

When our focus is on material things, what we possess, what we "deserve," and how well our situation compares to someone else's, then we destroy our potential for true happiness.

I went to an important University of Louisville basketball

game a few years ago. I knew I was privileged to be there because the game had been sold out and people were outside the gate wanting to buy tickets. I sat down in my seat and thought, *Russell, you are so blessed to have this ticket and get to see this game. This is fun.* Then I looked across the arena and saw one of our associate ministers seated on the other side, at midcourt, in the best seat in the house. I began thinking, *What's he doing there? Who's he with? Why didn't they ask me? This seat is so far away, and that guy in front of me has a big head that blocks my view.* My happiness was lessened because of my envy. How ridiculous!

ENVY DESTROYS RELATIONSHIPS

While Ahab was pouting, his wife came in. Enter the original wicked queen—Jezebel. She asked him, "Why are you so sullen? Why won't you eat?"

Ahab must have curled his bottom lip as he said through sniffles, "Because I said to Naboth the Jezreelite, 'Sell me your vineyard; or if you prefer, I will give you another vineyard in its place.' But he said, 'I will not give you my vineyard'" (1 Kings 21:5–6).

Jezebel said, "Is this how you act as king over Israel? Get up and eat! Cheer up. I'll get you the vineyard of Naboth the Jezreelite" (1 Kings 21:7).

She corrected Ahab's attitude, but for all the wrong reasons. Jezebel was so evil she felt her husband should not be denied anything, regardless of the cost. "What are you pouting for?" she asked. "You ought to act like a king, and get yourself whatever it is you want. But since you are such a wimp, I'll do it for you."

Jezebel arranged for two false witnesses to testify that Naboth had cursed God and the king, both capital offenses. Naboth was dragged outside the city and stoned to death on those charges. Jezebel came back and said, "OK, Ahab. The vineyard is all yours. Naboth is dead." (See 1 Kings 21:15.)

Murder has a way of irrevocably damaging your relationship

with your neighbor. Do you remember a few years ago when the mother of a cheerleader plotted to kill the mother of another cheerleader? She was competitive and envious, and she wanted to make sure her daughter made the squad.

We wouldn't dream of hiring a hit man and arranging for the death of one we envy, but we will assassinate him verbally. Like Giotto's picture of envy, we have vicious tongues. We can destroy people with our gossip, sarcastic remarks, and petty arguments that stem from the envy in our souls.

Even the disciples of Jesus struggled with envy and bitter rivalries. Two ambitious brothers, James and John, once came to Jesus and had the audacity to say, "Jesus, when you sit on your throne some day, we would like to sit beside you—one on the right, the other on the left" (see Mark 10:37). James and John had no idea how wrong they were about the future kingdom of God. Jesus would not set up an earthly throne and reign like any other king. His would be a heavenly kingdom, where service and humility were rewarded.

You would hope that James and John were the only disciples who misunderstood. But when the other ten disciples heard about the brazenness of James and John, they were upset. They too wanted the important seats. How dare those brothers try to one-up everybody else. How unfair!

I would have lost patience with the disciples, but Jesus used it as an opportunity to teach how his kingdom would be different from the world of envy and greed. He said, "You know that those who are regarded as rulers of the Gentiles lord it over them, and their high officials exercise authority over them. Not so with you. Instead, whoever wants to become great among you must be your servant, and whoever wants to be first must be slave of all. For even the Son of Man did not come to be served, but to serve, and to give his life as a ransom for many" (Mark 10:42–45).

Several years ago a drunk driver crossed the median on

Interstate 71 near Carrollton, Kentucky, and plowed into a school bus loaded with children returning to our area from an amusement park in Cincinnati. Dozens of children and sponsors were killed in the explosion that followed. Our community was devastated and mourned with the families.

Recently our local paper related that five years after the accident, some of the victims' families have received sizable insurance settlements, but their neighbors have been resentful of their newfound wealth. Siblings of those who died are even hearing catty remarks like, "I bet you're glad your sister died because now you're rich and you think you're better than everybody else."

You can see why the apostle Paul pleaded with us, "Let us not become conceited, provoking and envying each other" (Galatians 5:26). Envy has a way of destroying relationships and alienating us from those around us.

Author Steven Covey tells of spending a cold evening entertaining his two young sons outside. He noticed that his four-year-old was shivering in the cold, so he removed his own jacket, wrapped it around his little boy, and cuddled him next to his chest to get him warm.

Later that night, when Covey tucked the older brother in bed, he sensed that his normally exuberant six-year-old was pouting. Covey asked his son a few questions, but the boy gave only one-word answers and turned to face the wall. Covey leaned over to get a better look at his son's face and saw tears in his eyes. "Son, what's wrong?" he asked.

With a quivering lip, his son replied, "Daddy, if I were cold, would you put your coat around me too?"

Our hearts sink when we picture Covey's little boy questioning his father's love. Likewise, how much pain we cause ourselves and our Father when we worry about how the Father is treating everybody else and we question whether he is treating us fairly. It must break his heart.

ENVY RENDERS GOD'S JUDGMENT

God appeared to Elijah the prophet and told him to confront the wicked Ahab, who was in Naboth's vineyard, taking possession of it. God told Elijah, "Say to [Ahab], 'This is what the LORD says: Have you not murdered a man and seized his property?' Then say to him, 'This is what the LORD says: In the place where dogs licked up Naboth's blood, dogs will lick up your blood—yes, yours!'" (1 Kings 21:19).

Elijah did what God commanded and went to see Ahab. When he faced the king, "Ahab said to Elijah, 'So you have found me, my enemy!'

"'I have found you,' he answered, 'because you have sold yourself to do evil in the eyes of the LORD. "I am going to bring disaster on you. I will consume your descendants and cut off from Ahab every last male in Israel—slave or free. I will make your house like that of Jeroboam son of Nebat and that of Baasha son of Ahijah, because you have provoked me to anger and have caused Israel to sin."

"'And also concerning Jezebel the LORD says: "Dogs will devour Jezebel by the wall of Jezreel"'" (1 Kings 21:20–23).

Ahab later went into battle and disguised himself so the enemy wouldn't try to assassinate him. But a random arrow hit Ahab between the sections of his armor, and he died later that day. Then, as Elijah had predicted, "They washed the chariot at a pool in Samaria…and the dogs licked up his blood, as the word of the LORD had declared" (1 Kings 22:38).

The wicked queen Jezebel also died a grizzly death. When Jehu was anointed king of Israel, he went to Jezreel to visit Queen Jezebel. She didn't know if he was coming in peace, but the chances weren't good because she had been so wicked.

When Jezebel heard about it, she painted her eyes, arranged her hair and looked out of a window. As Jehu entered the gate, she asked, "Have you come in peace, Zimri, you murderer of your master?"

He looked up at the window and called out, "Who is on my side? Who?" Two or three eunuchs looked down at him. "Throw her down!" Jehu said. So they threw her down, and some of her blood spattered the wall and the horses as they trampled her underfoot.

Jehu went in and ate and drank. "Take care of that cursed woman," he said, "and bury her, for she was a king's daughter." But when they went out to bury her, they found nothing except her skull, her feet and her hands. They went back and told Jehu, who said, "This is the word of the LORD that he spoke through his servant Elijah the Tishbite: On the plot of ground at Jezreel dogs will devour Jezebel's flesh." (2 Kings 9:30–36)

The person who gives in to his envy sins against God and will reap God's judgment. While we usually consider envy a "respectable" sin, the New Testament lists envy among the worst of sins: "The acts of the sinful nature are obvious: sexual immorality, impurity and debauchery; idolatry and witchcraft; hatred, discord, jealousy, fits of rage, selfish ambition, dissensions, factions and *envy*; drunkenness, orgies, and the like. I warn you, as I did before, that those who live like this will not inherit the kingdom of God" (Galatians 5:19–21, emphasis added).

We can be thankful that Christians are under grace and our sins are forgiven, but sin always leaves a scar. Ahab repented before God, but the scars were still there. He could not bring Naboth back from the grave.

ENVY IS SENSELESS

Ultimately, comparing ourselves to others makes no sense. God doesn't compare people to each other. He loves each of us for who we are and accepts us with all of our imperfections. He certainly wants us to be obedient to his Word because he has given us commands to protect us and provide for us the most meaningful life possible on this earth as well as eternal life. God does not, however, grade on a curve. He loves all of us unconditionally, regardless of how good or rich we are compared to someone else.

Therefore, it's foolish for us to envy someone who has more than we do. In the eternal scheme it doesn't matter whether someone had a little more money than someone else, or was a little more talented or a little better looking or a little better athlete. It doesn't matter if someone is a lot better in those areas. What matters is what we do with the talents and abilities God has given us; what matters most is who we are, not what we accomplish.

Paul wrote about how foolish we are when we fall into the comparison trap. He said, "We do not dare to classify or compare ourselves with some who commend themselves. When they measure themselves by themselves and compare themselves with themselves, they are not wise" (2 Corinthians 10:12).

As difficult as it is for me to remember, I am not in competition with Charles Swindoll or Bill Hybels or Charles Stanley. I want to be a better minister of God next year than I am now, and I think God honors that ambition. Regardless, God accepts me and loves me unconditionally just the way I am.

Accepting what God has given us as sufficient is one key to avoiding the comparison trap. Longtime preacher J. Wallace Hamilton told of a farmer who became discontented with his farm. He griped about the lake he had to walk around, the hills he had to climb, and the fat cows that never did what he wanted them to do. He griped about being so far from everything and how much upkeep the farm required each day.

Finally he decided to sell it and find a place more to his liking. He made plans to list it with a Realtor. A few days later, the Realtor telephoned, wanting him to approve an advertisement for the local paper. The advertisement described a farm in the ideal location—quiet and peaceful, with a beautiful landscape, fresh lakes, well-kept buildings, and well-bred livestock. The farmer said, "Read that ad to me again." After hearing it the second time, he said, "I've changed my mind. I'm not going to sell. I've been looking for a place like that all my life!"

CHAPTER FIVE

FOUR WAYS TO OVERCOME THE TRAPS

A good name is more desirable than great riches;
to be esteemed is better than silver or gold.
PROVERBS 22:1

Keep your lives free from the love of money and be content with
what you have, because God has said, "Never will I leave you;
never will I forsake you."
HEBREWS 13:5

I heard a preacher tell of sitting on a plane beside a young executive who was obviously depressed. When the young man learned he was sitting next to a minister, he began pouring out his heart. He said, "My goal in life was to become a millionaire by the time I was thirty-five. I had nothing to start with, but I reached my goal. I am a millionaire.

"But my life is not right," he said. "I don't communicate well with my kids. They're in trouble and they're snobs. My wife is threatening to leave me because I've not paid attention to her." He concluded, "I have spent my life climbing the ladder of success. Now I get to the top and discover the ladder is leaning against the wrong wall."

If we intend to honor God in the way we handle our finances, we must first change our thinking about money. There are four attitudes we must adopt to overcome the financial traps and to correctly align our perspective with God's principles.

ATTITUDE 1: PURSUE SPIRITUAL RICHES

Two ladies sitting near me on a plane were looking out the window as we were about to land. "Look," one of them said, "a shopping center!"

"There's another one!" the other chimed in.

I, on the other hand, look for golf courses.

We all have our areas of pursuit. Paul commanded Timothy, "Some people, eager for money, have wandered from the faith and pierced themselves with many griefs. But you, man of God, flee from all this, and pursue righteousness, godliness, faith, love, endurance and gentleness. Fight the good fight of the faith. Take hold of the eternal life to which you were called when you made your good confession in the presence of many witnesses" (1 Timothy 6:10–12). He was admonishing Timothy not to get caught up in running after temporary things but to pursue things that are worth capturing: righteousness, godliness, faith....

We need to remind ourselves of these priorities every day because we are surrounded by people who don't share these values. Daily we battle the world's brainwashing—a constant barrage of advertisements claiming we would be much happier if we had more things. The apostle Paul says, however, that the pursuit of possessions can wound us with many griefs.

How do we keep our perspective on eternal riches? Without minimizing the struggle, let me suggest there are four simple ways to keep our focus on godly pursuits. We can:

- Worship regularly to remind ourselves who is God.
- Begin each day with a quiet time in which we restate our pledge to God that he will come first in our lives and vow to remain humble before him.
- Cultivate relationships with other Christians who share our values.

- Avoid overexposure to advertisements; turn off the television occasionally and turn away from the constant enticement to buy more products.

The pursuit of money breeds pride; the pursuit of spiritual riches breeds humility. If we daily pursue righteousness, we are much less likely to become arrogant, regardless of our possessions. I remember looking across the congregation at one of our Christmas Eve services a couple of years ago and seeing a young man who had recently sold his business at a profit of several million dollars. As I watched him sitting on the floor with his two children, joyfully singing Christmas carols, an Old Testament passage came to mind: "This is what the LORD says: 'Let not the wise man boast of his wisdom or the strong man boast of his strength or the rich man boast of his riches, but let him who boasts boast about this: that he understands and knows me, that I am the LORD, who exercises kindness, justice and righteousness on earth, for in these I delight,' declares the LORD" (Jeremiah 9:23–24).

Notice, there's a difference between being rich and pursuing riches. It's not wrong to be rich. Many of the godly heroes of the Old Testament were wealthy men—David, Solomon, and Joseph, to name a few. Jesus had companions who were rich. Lazarus apparently owned a large home where Jesus stayed with his disciples. Mary, the sister of Lazarus, anointed Jesus with an expensive perfume. Zacchaeus had enough to give away half his resources when he met Jesus, and Jesus commended his generosity even though he didn't give away everything he had.

Though it's not wrong to be rich, it's foolish to make riches our life pursuit. Paul told Timothy, "Command those who are rich in this present world not to…put their hope in wealth, which is so uncertain, but to put their hope in God" (1 Timothy 6:17). Don't pursue something that is so uncertain.

Remember, It's Only Paper

In May 1987 a book hit the stores with an eye-catching title: *Blood in the Streets*. The authors, James Davidson and Lord William Rees-Mogg, have respectable résumés in the financial world. Despite their credentials, however, their book was given anything but a respectable reception by the critics. In some circles it was ridiculed because it made predictions that many considered to be wildly improbable. Their forecasts included the following:

- A major crash in the American stock market, which hit a few months later, in October 1987.
- A collapse in the financial assets boom in Japan, which occurred in 1990 and was a steeper decline than the American stock market crash of 1929.
- A decline in real-estate values worldwide. Within five years the world's largest property developers were headed for bankruptcy.

If that wasn't daring enough, their political forecasts seemed even more laughable:

- Despite its outward appearance of strength, communism was at death's door. Two years later the Berlin Wall came down and the Eastern European communist governments collapsed, one after another.
- The collapse of communism would lead to the breakup of the Soviet Union into its ethnic components. The world watched in shock as the Soviet Union died unexpectedly and swiftly.

The authors have followed with a sequel called *The Great Reckoning: Protecting Yourself in the Coming Depression*. They suggest that the collapse of communism has unleashed a tremendous deflationary force on the world. Cheap labor is available everywhere. Combine that with new technology, and tomorrow's goods will be produced so inexpensively that our world will never be the same.

No one knows if they will be right again. They will not always be able to accurately predict the future, but their writings do underscore the uncertainty of riches.

Wealth is deceptive because it masquerades as a source of stability. In reality, it is unreliable. Inflation, government intervention, military vulnerability, and even natural disasters can add to its unpredictability.

One of the most uncertain sources of income is Social Security. It is now being suggested that the retirement age be raised to seventy so that the Social Security program can survive. Dorcas Hardy, the former head of Social Security under Ronald Reagan and George Bush, was so appalled at what she discovered about the program that she wrote a book entitled *Social Insecurity*.

There is little security in wealth of any kind. Ecclesiastes 5:10 warns, "Whoever loves money never has money enough; whoever loves wealth is never satisfied with his income. This too is meaningless." Famines can come at any time. We might lose our job, we could become disabled, our parents might become ill, or the stock market could crash.

Sam Walton made millions of dollars a year for the last several years of his life. He was reputed to be the second wealthiest man in America. Just before his death, his Wal-Mart chain passed Sears to become the number-one retail store in America. In the midst of his prosperity, Walton maintained a reputation for being an honest and generous man and an outspoken Christian.

When the stock market took its dive in 1987, Walton was informed that he had lost over one billion dollars in one day. He shrugged and said, "It's only paper."[1] You may be tempted to think that's easy to say when you have so much money, but without a godly perspective, people will put their trust in their wealth. When it proves to be vulnerable, many people panic. Only by recognizing beforehand the uncertainty of riches will we be prepared to respond with confidence, as Sam Walton did, when our wealth fails to be trustworthy.

If you are caught up in the mindless rat race of this world, sacrificing your time and energy to accumulate as many things as possible, STOP. Change your goals. It's not worth sacrificing your happiness, your friends, and your eternity for a few trinkets in this life. Refocus your ambitions. Remind yourself that it is not your goal to be rich. Paul said, "Set your minds on things above, not on earthly things" (Colossians 3:2). Replace your ambition for worldly things with a desire for an eternal life with God. Learn to be even more enthusiastic about serving than you have been about accumulating.

Don't Settle for Less than the Best

C. S. Lewis said that the problem is not that we want good things for ourselves. It's not really wrong to desire our own good and hope for enjoyment. He explained, "Indeed, if we consider the staggering nature of the rewards promised in the Gospels, it would seem that our Lord finds our desires not too strong, but too weak. We are halfhearted creatures, fooling about with drink and sex and ambition when infinite joy is offered us, like an ignorant child who wants to go on making mud pies in a slum because he cannot imagine what is meant by the offer of a holiday at the sea. We are far too easily pleased."

Our problem is not that we are too ambitious, but that our ambition is misdirected. We are willing to settle for a house, a nice car, a television or two, a microwave, and an occasional evening of entertainment. We have conditioned ourselves to settle for such meager, short-lived pleasures that our capacity for the eternal has shriveled. Christ calls us to set our affections on things above, to lay up treasure in eternity, and to be ambitious for that which has real significance in life. God pleads with us, "Why spend money on what is not bread, and your labor on what does not satisfy? Listen, listen to me, and eat what is good, and your soul will delight in the richest of fare" (Isaiah 55:2).

The Book of Proverbs lists five things that are more important than money:

- *Reputation:* "A good name is more desirable than great riches; to be esteemed is better than silver or gold" (Proverbs 22:1).
- *Wisdom:* "Blessed is the man who finds wisdom, the man who gains understanding, for she is more profitable than silver and yields better returns than gold. She is more precious than rubies; nothing you desire can compare with her" (Proverbs 3:13–15).
- *Integrity:* "Buy the truth and do not sell it; get wisdom, discipline and understanding" (Proverbs 23:23).
- *Intelligence:* "Gold there is, and rubies in abundance, but lips that speak knowledge are a rare jewel" (Proverbs 20:15).
- *Harmonious relationships:* "Better a meal of vegetables where there is love than a fattened calf with hatred" (Proverbs 15:17).

Jesus added salvation to the list, saying, "What good is it for a man to gain the whole world, yet forfeit his soul?" (Mark 8:36). Most of us would add good health, freedom, and happiness to the list of things that are more important than money.

God may bless you financially, but he wants so much more for you than just worldly riches, which are so uncertain. Instead of pursuing something fragile, determine that you will honor God by pursuing "righteousness, godliness, faith, love, endurance and gentleness." Instead of fighting to get to the top of the success ladder or to grab hold of a brass ring that will some day fade away, "fight the good fight of the faith" and "take hold of the eternal life to which you were called" (1 Timothy 6:11–12).

ATTITUDE 2: HANDLE YOUR MONEY WITH INTEGRITY

A few years ago some drug dealers approached the captain of an oil tanker that regularly made trips from South America to Los Angeles. The dealers offered the captain $10,000 if he would bring a load of cocaine into America. He refused.

They came back again, offering $50,000 cash for one load. He again refused.

They returned a third time and asked if he would do it for $150,000. He said he would think about it. Instead, he called the FBI. The authorities put together a sting operation, and it worked perfectly. They caught the drug dealers and seized a shipment of drugs, $350,000 in cash, and a list of buyers in the Los Angeles area.

After the incident, one of the federal agents asked the captain, "Why did you wait until they offered $150,000 before calling us?"

"They were getting pretty close to my price, and I was scared," he answered.

Money can be such a strong temptation, and Satan will use it to his advantage. If we do not determine to handle all financial decisions with honesty and integrity, then envy and greed will get the best of us, and we will fall. The psalmist wrote, "Let not my heart be drawn to what is evil, to take part in wicked deeds with men who are evildoers; let me not eat of their delicacies" (Psalm 141:4).

US News & World Report in June 1996 reported the following staggering statistics that reveal how the pursuit of riches can lead to dishonesty, cheating, and stealing.

More and more folks will commit crime or sacrifice clear-cut ethical norms for money. If there were such a thing as an index of leading greed indicators, it would have shown sharp increases in categories like these:

Health care fraud amounts to $100 billion a year. The most common scams: billing for services not rendered and ordering unnecessary medical procedures. People justify ripping off insurance companies and government-run health programs like Medicare and Medicaid because what they do is seen as a "victimless crime," argues James Garcia, the former head of the fraud unit at Aetna Insurance. He says such theft has worsened in recent years as cost-saving pressures on doctors and hospitals grow, and he suspects they want to make up their lost incomes.

The Association of Certified Fraud Examiners reports that about $435 billion is ripped off from businesses by their own workers each year—about 6 percent of an average firm's revenues and three times the estimated rate of such fraud in the 1960s.

Besides health care programs, people defraud other government agencies with impunity. About 25 percent of Americans admit to some form of tax cheating, and that costs $100 billion annually, says M. Hisch Goldberg in his book *The Complete Book of Greed.* And fraud in the workers' compensation programs hit an estimated $5 billion in 1995, according to the National Insurance Crime Bureau.

The Josephson Institute's "1996 Report Card on American Integrity" found that in the past five years stealing by teens had increased. Now, some 42 percent of teen boys and 31 percent of teen girls admitted stealing something at least once last year.

Beyond actual crimes, there is plenty of evidence many folks would follow money down the wrong path.

A study in the February issue of the *Journal of Business Ethics* found that 47 percent of top executives and 76 percent of graduate-level business students say they would commit fraud by understating their firms' write-offs against profits, especially if the chance for a job promotion was linked to higher profit figures. Similarly, in surveys of lawyers, Cumberland School of Law Prof. William Ross has found that 40 percent of lawyers admitted that the prospect of billing time had sometimes influenced their decision to proceed with work that they weren't sure was necessary.[2]

Determine that the green-eyed monster is not going to get the best of you. Make a commitment to tell the truth, no matter what the financial cost. That takes courage and integrity. You may lose the respect of your peers. You may lose your job. But you will gain respect for yourself and honor in the eyes of God.

Decide that character is going to be more important to you than financial status or self-esteem. Otherwise, you risk losing all three. Make a commitment to handle all financial affairs with honesty. A good place to begin is with the following promises to yourself and God:

- I will not cheat anyone.
- I will not lie, even in the smallest way, to anyone.
- I will not manipulate others or treat them unjustly.
- I will pay my bills on time.
- I will pay my taxes.
- I will pay my employees what I promised them.
- I will not lie about where I spent my money.
- I will not lie on my income tax return, my résumé, or my insurance claim form.
- I will refuse to exaggerate the worth of my product or manipulate someone into buying something he doesn't want.

• I will make an honest profit and will be fair to those who helped me make it.

ATTITUDE 3: BE HAPPY WITH SIMPLICITY

When our two sons were in elementary school, my church softball team qualified for a tournament in York, Pennsylvania. We knew we wouldn't be far from Washington, D.C., and many other historical sights that our children had never seen. Although we couldn't afford to take an extravagant vacation, we decided to save and scrimp so our boys could see some of America's heritage. We decided to stay in inexpensive motels, eat bologna or peanut butter and jelly sandwiches for lunch, go to inexpensive fast-food restaurants for supper, then buy donuts and milk in the evening so we could eat breakfast in the motel room.

We went to the FBI building, to Gettysburg, to the White House, and the Smithsonian Institute. We had a great time. On the long trip home, we began passing the time by recalling what we had done each day. I could tell the boys had really enjoyed themselves, so I was curious to know what had been their favorite part of the trip.

"Of all the things we got to do, what was your favorite?" I asked them.

They both agreed it was when we had gone to a park and eaten sandwiches, then walked down by the lake to feed the ducks. I thought I had creatively provided all this extravagant entertainment, and they were the most satisfied with the simplest event of the week!

The older we get and the wealthier we become, the harder it is to be happy with the simple things. We think we deserve the best, not just the basics. Once you have stayed at the Hyatt, it's difficult to be content with Motel 6. Once you have flown to an exotic vacation spot overseas, it's hard to be content vacationing in the state park. Once you've driven a Mercedes, it's hard to drive a

Chevette. But a wise Christian disciplines himself to expect only the basics and be thankful for them. Anything above that is a double blessing.

It is especially difficult to be content with simplicity in such an age of prosperity. One sociologist revealed that in 1900 the average American wanted seventy-two different things and considered eighteen of them essential. Today the average person in America wants five hundred things and considers one hundred of them essential.

Someone has said, "Who is happier—the man with six children or the man with six million dollars? It is the man with six children because the man with six million dollars wants more!" The secret to happiness is not in having many things but in believing that what you have is enough. Epicurus said, "Wealth consists not in having great possessions but in few wants."

We know things don't satisfy, but it's a lesson we sometimes learn the hard way. A friend of mine, Ron Decker, had always wanted a Corvette. The only problem was that he was a school-teacher, and money was a little scarce. But he saved until he was able to buy a new Corvette. He was so proud of that car.

Soon Ron discovered that owning a Corvette wasn't as fulfilling as he had thought. He feared someone parking next to him and putting a dent in his doors, so he would double park in parking lots. People gave him dirty looks and even left nasty notes on his windshield. Then he began to park in the back of the lots, where no one was beside him. He didn't mind walking the extra distance, but he began worrying that someone might try to steal the car, so he bought an alarm system. Predictably, the alarm went off several times in the middle of the night, angering his neighbors. It wasn't long before he got sick of all the hassles and sold the Corvette.

The person who can learn to be content with the simple things, even if he can afford more, honors God and enjoys life.

My friend Jimmy Dan Conner is a former University of Kentucky basketball star. He once said to me, "Find two guys, and we'll go watch the UK game this week in Lexington." I took two of our staff members, both avid Kentucky fans. Jimmy Dan had two season tickets on the third row of the arena, and he had been given two other seats, which he thought would be nearby, but they were in the upper deck. During the first half, I sat with him in the good seats, knowing my two coworkers were happy just to be in the arena.

With about five minutes left in the first half, Jimmy Dan said, "Let's exchange seats with Mike and Jim for the second half." We did, but it was harder to be content up there. The game was just a rumor. There weren't even backs on the seats. I heard fans around me buzzing, "What's Jimmy Dan Conner doing sitting up here?" People with Jimmy Dan's clout just don't sit up there. I was impressed with Jimmy Dan's humble willingness to accept the lesser seats.

Jesus said: "When someone invites you to a wedding feast, do not take the place of honor, for a person more distinguished than you may have been invited. If so, the host who invited both of you will come and say to you, 'Give this man your seat.' Then, humiliated, you will have to take the least important place. But when you are invited, take the lowest place, so that when your host comes, he will say to you, 'Friend, move up to a better place.' Then you will be honored in the presence of all your fellow guests. For everyone who exalts himself will be humbled, and he who humbles himself will be exalted" (Luke 14:8–11).

A South Vietnamese author was imprisoned by the Vietcong for several years during the Vietnam War. After his release he wrote *The Vietnamese Gulag*, a book about his prison experiences. He related an old Vietnamese tale about a family of twelve who lived in a one-room house. When the father got tired of listening to the complaints about the house being so crowded, he brought the horse into the house and left him there. After a week, he took the horse away, and everyone was ecstatic about the amount of room they had taken for granted before.

He said it was the same in prison in Vietnam. The more freedom they took away, the less his desires demanded. When he was first in prison, he shouted and maintained his innocence. He demanded an apology and screamed that he should be released. Time passed, and he entered the second stage. He would think, *If they would just kick me in the pants hard and release me, I would take that.* Then a third stage came when he grew weary of the sandy rice he had to eat, and he was convinced that happiness would be a little bit of meat or a little bit of sugar. Then in the fourth stage he thought, *Forget the meat and sugar; just give me someone to talk to.* In the next stage, he said he decided that "joy would be if I had my hands free and my legs unshackled so I could sit up and walk even three paces." He concluded, "I reached the point where getting a clean cotton T-shirt and a new pair of shorts was the height of ecstasy."

Contentment has so little to do with how much we have. It has everything to do with our expectations and our attitude. Here are two practical suggestions for developing and maintaining an attitude of contentment.

Express Kindness to Those You Envy

Instead of churning inside about the people who appear to have it better than you, pray for them. When you begin to envy a person, pray that God will bless him. Then do something compassionate for him. Send a note of congratulations to the businessman who succeeds. Compliment a friend who was given a beautiful diamond ring. Send a housewarming gift to the couple who just bought a bigger house than yours. Be willing to "rejoice with those who rejoice" (Romans 12:15), and you will begin sharing in the greater riches of friendship instead of being shriveled up with envy.

I had the privilege of meeting Joe Liedke recently. Joe Liedke grew up in Northwestern Pennsylvania near my hometown and played basketball against my brother in high school. About the same time I began my ministry in Louisville, Kentucky, in the midsixties, Liedke came to the University of Louisville and became their starting center. Although I didn't know him then, I admired him from a distance because of his attitude when all-American Wes Unseld came to Louisville and stole the starting position from him. I remember his saying, "It's an honor to support an all-American like Wes Unseld." That's class. He could have succumbed to temptation and been envious and resentful. Instead, he expressed kindness to the one who had been given more.

Years ago I took my older son with me to a men's retreat in Indiana where I was one of two speakers. The other minister spoke on Friday night, and I was to speak on Saturday. On Friday night he was terrific. He was articulate, humorous, and convicting. At the end of his speech, he used a moving illustration that left all the men in tears.

When we returned to our room after the service, I was thinking about my assignment for Saturday morning and battling envy. I didn't want to follow that excellent speaker and be compared to him. What if my jokes bombed? What if my stories didn't leave them in tears? Would my message seem boring after such a moving sermon the night before? I didn't want everyone talking about how great the Friday night speaker was and leaving me out.

My twelve-year-old son broke the silence and said, "Dad, that guy was good. And you have to speak at the next meeting tomorrow morning?"

"Yeah, do you think I'm in trouble?" I asked.

He said, "Well, Dad, they're pretty spoiled!"

That's not what I expected him to say! I wanted him to say, "Oh, Dad, you're every bit as good a speaker as he is." But he was no help.

That night I prayed about my envy. "Lord, I'm envious," I confessed. "I'm looking to criticize. I'm comparing. Forgive me and help me to have the right spirit. Help me to do the best I can with the gift you gave me. Use both of us for your glory."

The next morning I introduced myself to the previous night's speaker and complimented him on the message he had delivered. I said, "That's the first time I've ever heard you preach. It was outstanding. You have a wonderful gift from God."

To my surprise he responded, "That really means something coming from you, Bob. I've admired you for a long time." After that, it was hard to be envious of someone with so much perception! It was much easier for me to be content with the role I had been given.

Count Your Blessings

One of the elders in our church, Bill Beauchamp, was once involved in a serious automobile accident just two days before Christmas. He had a broken arm and was banged up badly. His daughter, who was also in the car, was bruised but not seriously injured. I went to visit Bill in the hospital and expected him to be really down. Having to spend Christmas Day in a hospital room was certainly reason for depression. It was a surprise when, from his hospital bed, Bill said to me, "Bob, this is the greatest Christmas of my life. I'm so thankful to be alive. Sherry could have been seriously hurt. She's OK, and I'm going to be fine. I have so much to be grateful for!"

Several years ago two children were selling Christmas cards door-to-door in a middle-class neighborhood in Cincinnati, Ohio. One mother invited them in so they could get warm, then brought them hot chocolate and cookies. The two children were wide-eyed as they gawked at everything in the room. "Are you rich?" they asked.

The woman grinned as she thought to herself, *Rich? We own*

an average house and a car, we have a MasterCard payment that gives us fits...

Before she could say anything, one of the kids said, "Lady, you must be rich. Your cups and saucers match!"

Do you remember the old hymn "Count Your Blessings"?

When upon life's billows you are tempest tossed,
When you are discouraged, thinking all is lost,
Count your many blessings, name them one by one,
And it will surprise you what the Lord has done.

When you look at others with their lands and gold,
Think that Christ has promised you his wealth untold.
Count your many blessings—Money cannot buy
Your reward in heaven, or your home on high.

Count your blessings, name them one by one,
Count your many blessings, see what God has done!

When we count our blessings, we cannot help but be humbled by and grateful for God's generosity to us.

ATTITUDE 4: FACE YOUR MORTALITY

According to the verse, "we brought nothing into the world, and we can take nothing out of it" (1 Timothy 6:7). But some people refuse to believe they can't take it with them. A few years ago I read an article about a woman whose final request to her husband was that he bury her with her car, a 1976 Cadillac in mint condition. He purchased fourteen burial plots to accommodate her final request. The vault for the car was twenty-seven feet by twelve feet by six feet. The picture in the newspaper showed a crane lowering her car into the vault with the caption, "She did take it with her!"

I heard about a rich man who was equally determined to take it with him. He told his wife to get all of his money together and put it in a sack, then hang the sack from the rafters in the attic. He said, "When I die and my spirit is caught up to heaven, I'll seize the sack on the way by." He later died, and the woman raced up to the attic, only to find the sack still there. "I knew I should have put the sack in the basement!" she said.

Perhaps nothing brings out our true character like facing our own mortality. Have you ever talked with a skillful life insurance salesman? He usually refuses to come right out and say you're going to die. "If something unfortunate should happen to you, God forbid," he will say.

Sometimes I laugh and respond, "Hey, I'm going to die some day. God isn't going to forbid it; he's going to welcome it! Isn't that why you're here, because you know I'm going to die some day? Let's talk about what preparations I need to make for *when* I die."

The apostle Paul was right when he said, "we brought nothing into the world, and we can take nothing out of it." (You probably hadn't realized Paul was the first one to say, "You can't take it with you.") Newborn babies bring nothing with them when they arrive in this world. They don't come with a five-thousand-dollar certificate of deposit to cover their expenses. They wear no diamonds on their fingers. They're stark naked and flat broke. When we die, we will take nothing with us. That may be humbling, but it is the truth.

I mentioned earlier the popular bumper sticker that reads, "He who dies with the most toys wins." I saw a T-shirt at a Christian gathering that had a great response: "He who dies with the most toys...still dies." No matter how much money you have, you still cannot conquer death. Howard Hughes died. Cornelius Vanderbilt died. John D. Rockefeller died. Jacqueline Kennedy Onassis died.

A few years ago on vacation our family started playing

Monopoly late one night. It was one of those nights when everything was going my way. The first time around the board I stopped on Illinois Avenue and Park Place. The next time around I got Indiana and Kentucky Avenues. I bought Boardwalk and soon owned all four railroads. I put houses and then hotels on every street. I could see that, barring a disaster, I was going to win. My family members would stop on one of my properties, and I would smirk, "That's four hundred dollars." Later, "That's eight hundred dollars—I have a hotel there!" I could hardly keep from giggling. I accumulated cash and deeds and hotels. I was powerful.

About one o'clock in the morning, everyone went bankrupt and I finally won. They got up from the table without one word of congratulations and headed to bed. I said, "Wait, someone needs to put the game away."

They kept walking and said, "That's your reward for winning."

There I sat. My money, my hotels, my deeds, and my victory surrounded me, but I was all alone. I picked up my money and my hotels and my deeds and put them back in the box, closed the lid, and went upstairs to a cold bed. My wife didn't say, "I'm proud of you. You're so smart...you are Mr. Monopoly." She gave me a kiss good-night and turned to face the wall.

I lay there in the darkness, remembering that I had heard James Dobson compare life to a Monopoly game. We work hard to accumulate things so we can impress people who will probably resent us anyway. Then one day it's all over, we give it all back, and someone puts us in a box and closes the lid. Suddenly the dollar bills, deeds, and hotels don't matter. What matters is whether or not we pursued righteousness, godliness, faith, love, endurance, and gentleness. What matters is whether or not we are ready to face God.

I counted dollars while God counted crosses.
I counted gains while he counted losses.

I counted my worth, my things gained in store,
And he sized me up by the scars that I bore.
I counted honors and sought degrees,
He counted the hours I spent on my knees.
I never knew till one day by the grave
How vain are the things we spend our lives to save.

(SOURCE UNKNOWN)

■

PART 2

ESCAPING THE DEBT TRAP

CHAPTER SIX

Have You Fallen into the Debt Trap?

I'm working as hard as I can to get my life and my cash to run out at the same time. If I can die right after lunch on Tuesday, everything will be fine.

PROFESSIONAL GOLFER DOUG SANDERS

On September 1, 1996, the *Chicago Tribune* carried an article with the following headline: "Luck Ran Out Quickly for Lottery Millionaire."

"Buddy Post may be the unluckiest lucky man alive, living proof that money can't buy happiness," the article read. In 1988, Buddy Post won more than sixteen million dollars in the Pennsylvania Lottery, but since then his life has been anything but lucky.

In 1992, Post was forced to give one-third of his winnings to his former landlord, Ann Karpik, who said that she shared the lottery ticket with Post. He had trouble keeping up with the legal fees since he was blocked from receiving access to the winnings during the court battle. Neither could he afford the bills he incurred for the bar, used-car lot, and other failed business ventures he and his siblings began after his jackpot win.

In 1993, "Post's brother, Jeffrey, was convicted of plotting to kill Buddy and his wife, Constance…as part of a scheme to gain access to the lottery money," the article revealed.

By 1994, Post had filed for bankruptcy. His wife had filed for divorce. He was $500,000 in debt, not counting taxes and legal fees. He was trying to auction off the remaining lottery payments to pay his attorneys' fees, home mortgage, and other debts—and rid himself of the "lottery albatross."

"Money didn't change me," Post said. "It changed people around me that I knew, that I thought cared a little bit about me. But they only cared about the money."

When he was asked what he was going to do next, Post said, "I'm just going to stay at home and mind my P's and Q's. Money draws flies."

FALLING INTO THE DEBT TRAP

Unfortunately, many of us know what it's like to be in debt. Nearly one million Americans file for bankruptcy every year.[1] Thousands of others seek help through credit counseling because they are too far in debt to get out. More than 25 percent of the average family's income goes to debt retirement, not including their home mortgages. Four out of five of us owe more than we own.[2]

Chances are good that even you have fallen into the debt trap at least once in your life, or perhaps you or a loved one is struggling to get out right now.

Do you often feel you can't save for the future as you would like?

Do you think you can't afford to give to the church as you know you should?

Do you have trouble relaxing and enjoying life because of financial pressures?

Then you have fallen into the debt trap.

Take comfort. There is a way of getting—and staying—out. And a trip to a pigpen may be the place to begin.

In Luke 15, Jesus told the parable about the lost, or prodigal, son. In this story, a young man couldn't wait for his father to die before he received his share of the inheritance. Instead, he talked his father into giving him his portion ahead of time so he could be on his own. The son then ran off to a far country, where he wasted all his money on wild living. Before long, he found himself forced to work on a pig farm in order to eat. There he sobered up and began to question how he got himself into such a financial mess.

The prodigal son made several mistakes on his way to the pigsty, the same mistakes we often make on our way to the debt trap.

OVERESTIMATING THE IMPORTANCE OF WEALTH

Evidently the prodigal son had fantasized for some time about what it would be like to have all the wealth he was to inherit when his father died. Money became more important to him than his family relationships and his personal integrity. Finally he could stand it no longer. He went to his father and said, "I want my inheritance now. I'm tired of waiting for you to kick the bucket" (my paraphrase).

The first mistake a lot of us make on the way to financial trouble is overestimating the importance of money. We think money will solve our problems, bring us happiness, buy us friends, or make us important. In his book *Balancing the Tightrope,* Perry Powell relates the findings of a survey of two hundred thousand college freshman in which 76 percent listed financial prosperity as an essential or very important goal of life. Only 39 percent said it was important to develop a meaningful philosophy of life.

Older adults are no better. The number one issue in any presidential election is always the economy—not moral values, foreign policy, crime, or abortion, but money. Everyone wants to know what a presidential candidate will do for his pocketbook.

When the son ended up in the pigpen, he realized there were things in life more important than money. I'm sure he wished he could go back and undo all the damage he had done. Wasting his inheritance, ruining his relationship with his family, and eating with the pigs were high prices to pay for the momentary pleasures money had brought him.

WANTING INSTANT GRATIFICATION

"The younger one said to his father, 'Father, give me my share of the estate.' So he divided his property between them." (Luke 15:12)

The prodigal's first mistake easily led to his second one. Since he thought money and the things money could buy were so important, he thought he needed them all immediately. The inheritance was going to be his some day, and probably would have been more profitable, but he couldn't wait.

Someone has defined discipline as "the ability to postpone pleasure." We get ourselves into financial and spiritual difficulty when we cannot postpone pleasure till the proper time. Our desire for instant gratification leads to impulse buying, the easiest path to the debt trap.

The *Wall Street Journal* carried an article about the shocking spending habits of this generation, entitled "The American Way of Buying: Portrait of a Young Consumer Wastrel." Based on interviews with more than four thousand Americans, this article recounts how baby boomers grew up in an era of luxury. Their parents worked hard to obtain wealth. As children the boomers enjoyed the fruits of their parents' labors, and they are spoiled. They're tempted to think they're entitled to the same standard of living their parents have now, forgetting that it took their parents twenty-five years to get there. So young people today will routinely spend whole paychecks and more to reach for the highest living standard possible because they're accustomed to instant gratification. The author concluded that young consumers spend far too freely on "items for immediate pleasure."[3]

But boomers aren't the only ones susceptible to instant gratification. I heard an older man say his wife's credit cards were stolen but he hasn't reported it because the thieves are spending less than she was! However, despite the stereotypes, Larry Burkett, after years of financial counseling, determined that in actuality men are worse than women about spending money they don't have. Wives, he says, may buy impulsively, but husbands buy extravagantly! A woman might buy a new dress, but a man buys a new computer or a sports car or a boat—much more costly items that can get the family into prolonged problems.

Although I'm usually a reluctant buyer, I've made some silly purchases in my lifetime. I hate to admit that I've bought something I didn't need and never used, but I have—like the stairstep machine I bought for $350 a couple of years ago and have been on ten times.

Advertisers thrive on impulse buyers. The typical consumer is exposed to more than three hundred advertisements a day, many of them preaching the benefits of instant gratification and easy credit.

"Why wait?" they say. "Enjoy it now, pay later."

"You can drive it away today and not make your first payment for sixty days."

"For only $19.95 a month..."

"You can have easy installment payments."

The message is clear: Indulge yourself now and be instantly gratified because you deserve it! Few voices encourage us to live within our means and wait until we can afford it. Author Sylvia Porter said, "We feel we have to have things today that people did without altogether five years ago."

Grocery stores are masters at advertising. Don't ever go into a grocery store hungry if impulse buying is a temptation for you! Our associate minister Dave Stone says his wife won't let him go to the store anymore, even for one or two items, because he will come out with two armloads of groceries. "Well, I saw that bag of chips on sale," he will say. "And that candy bar near the register is my favorite. Then I knew we'd need something to drink with all these snacks."

The easiest way to avoid impulse buying is to follow this rule: Never buy something you didn't plan ahead of time to buy. If that's too difficult, at least refuse to spend more money than you planned to spend.

SPENDING ON SINFUL ACTIVITY

> [Jesus said,] "Not long after that, the younger son got together all he had, set off for a distant country and there squandered his wealth in wild living." (Luke 15:13)

The prodigal's exasperated brother would later describe this wild living by saying to his father, "This son of yours...has squandered your property with prostitutes" (Luke 15:30). Professor Marion Henderson nailed it when he said the young man spent his money on "wine, women and song—and not much on song!"

As the prodigal soon learned, sin is costly. Ultimately it brings pain with a price tag, because a sinful habit has not only financial, but more importantly, spiritual repercussions. There are three common areas where I've seen Christians squander their money and reap terrible spiritual and financial consequences.

Alcohol and Illegal Drugs

Think of the millions of dollars that are wasted on alcohol consumption each year. The toll on human lives, however, is even more costly: traffic deaths, birth defects, broken families, emotional and health problems. Drug habits have similar consequences, costing users as much as a hundred dollars a day—sometimes more. The perpetrators of violent crimes are almost always under the influence of alcohol or some other mind-altering drug. Proverbs 23:21

warns, "For drunkards and gluttons become poor, and drowsiness clothes them in rags."

Pornography

A counselor told me of one Christian couple who spent more than thirty-five hundred dollars a year on pornographic videos and literature. Pornography will destroy a person's marriage and his soul, as it wastes his money.

A simple solution? Don't make the first purchase. Pornography develops a continual lust for more exposure and more extreme depictions, until the interest becomes an addiction that is difficult to break. This addiction can lead to criminal activity, as indicated by statistics that nearly all violent sex crimes are committed by men addicted to pornography.[4]

Gambling

A few years ago the Pennsylvania State Lottery accumulated a $100 million prize. Two lottery machines were set up in the Pittsburgh Airport, and people flew in from as far away as California—paying as much as $750 in airfare—to purchase lottery tickets. Many returned home without ever leaving the airport. Yet the chances of winning were 1 in 9.6 million!

Ninety million people visit US casinos every year. Americans wager more than $480 billion a year in legal forms of gambling. By contrast, the cost to the country for the Persian Gulf War in 1990–91 was $100 billion.[5]

The apostle Paul said, "He who has been stealing must steal no longer, but must work, doing something useful with his own hands, that he may have something to share with those in need" (Ephesians 4:28). I'm not implying that buying a lottery ticket is stealing, but Paul's point goes deeper. A person of character should want to earn the money he is making. He should naturally desire to do something "useful" in exchange for his income. To perform a service, to create a product someone needs, or to invest money in the stock of someone's company helps not only us but the recipient of our work. Even a gift blesses both the recipient and the giver, if it is given voluntarily and out of a generous heart. For a person to gain in the lottery or other gambling ventures, someone else has to lose against his wishes. Actually a lot of people have to lose, and the vast majority of people involved in the lottery lose money. As Buddy Post proved, even the winners often lose.

Leaders of the Saint Malchy's Parish on the west side of Chicago wondered what influence the Illinois State Lottery was having on their parishioners. It was decided that on a designated Sunday the members of the parish would place their losing lottery tickets for that week in the offering plates. The church gathered more than five thousand dollars' worth of lottery tickets—quite a collection for a church whose average weekly offering was only three hundred dollars![6] Think what churches could do to help the poor and win souls if their members willingly gave what they formerly had spent on lottery tickets.

I have heard people claim that any money they win will be given to the church. They reason, "Think how much my church could use a million dollars!" But that is not good stewardship. The lottery exploits the poor, introduces people to the addiction of gambling, promotes an antibiblical attitude toward money, and wastes a family's resources.

Other forms of gambling, like betting on sporting events, buying a chance at a prize, or betting on a card game, may seem innocent enough on the surface. A person could argue that it can't be a sin to spend a dollar on a chance to win a prize, knowing the proceeds will support the local high school band or the cheerleaders—and he might be right. Someone else might claim that the two dollars he spends on a horse race is purely for fun and is actually pretty cheap entertainment. My personal conviction, however, is that gambling should be avoided altogether for these reasons:

- A person of character shouldn't risk his money hoping to gain something for nothing.
- A Christian shouldn't risk his money on something that will give him a return only if others lose money.
- Gambling is addictive. While we might be able to handle it, someone following our example might not.

A common thread in all three areas—alcohol, gambling, pornography—is addiction. We indulge ourselves one time for the pleasure or out of curiosity. Then the next time we have to do more to get the high. Sin never satisfies for long, and soon we may find ourselves addicted. Eventually we realize the pleasure we sought is bringing us pain, but we can't get out.

If you can look at your checkbook, credit card statement, or the receipts in your grocery bag and see proof that one of these addictions has you in its grip, don't ignore it. Seek help. Find a Christian counselor who can help you break out of your addiction. The first step toward freedom is admitting you have a problem you want to overcome.

In addition to the freedom from the sinful habit, think about the financial burdens that can be lifted. I have seen a man walk to the counter at a food mart and purchase a six-pack of beer, a carton of cigarettes, a *Playboy* magazine, and a five-dollar lottery ticket, for a total bill of twenty dollars. If he does that just once a week, he will spend more than one thousand dollars in the course of a year. (That doesn't take into account how much those things may cost him years later if they ruin his health or his marriage.) If he had invested that one thousand dollars a year, starting at the age of twenty-one, he could easily have saved well over one million dollars by the time he was sixty-five. Truly, sin doesn't pay!

NOT ANTICIPATING HARD TIMES

[Jesus said,] "After he had spent everything, there was a severe famine in that whole country." (Luke 15:14)

The prodigal hadn't counted on a famine. He acted as though things would continue as they always had and he would never run out of money. Instead, suddenly his money was gone, no one cared about anything but food, and he couldn't buy a loaf of bread. He was broke and hungry.

Like the prodigal, many of us have acted as though hard times were not a possibility. The American economy has been relatively stable for a long time, but rather than seeing that as a blessing from God, we have taken it for granted.

Financial advisers warn that as a result of having a deficit for too many years, the American economy is in a precarious state. We can expect a prolonged recession, they warn; the famine is coming. God may allow our economy to suffer periods of famine so we'll be reminded to trust in him (see Deuteronomy 28).

Even if the national economy remains stable, we need to anticipate occasional personal famines. The Bible says in James 4:13–14, "Now listen, you who say, 'Today or tomorrow we will go to this or that city, spend a year there, carry on business and make money.' Why, you do not even know what will happen tomorrow. What is your life? You are a mist that appears for a little while and then vanishes." We cannot predict the future. We may not anticipate doctor bills, children's braces, a pregnancy that takes away a second income, or a parent's illness. To assume things will always be as they are now is to put faith in our own ability to control the future and to ignore the warnings of God.

I'm not recommending we live our lives anticipating every possible crisis that could occur. We would end up spending too much on insurance—and on ulcer medication! We can trust that God will take care of us as he has promised, but a wise planner also allows for some of the famines that may appear in this life.

Larry Burkett says young couples often fail to anticipate famines and therefore make serious financial mistakes in their first two years of marriage—mistakes that will handicap them for years. The most common, he says, is purchasing a house based on two incomes. Rather than starting out with a smaller house and moving up as their income grows, they estimate their ability to pay on the assumption that they will always have both incomes. So they overextend themselves. When unexpected bills or babies come along, they find themselves unable to keep up the payments and begin spiraling into debt.[7]

SPENDING MORE THAN RESOURCES ALLOW

[Jesus said,] "After he had spent everything...he began to be in need." (Luke 15:14)

Someone has said, "If your outgo exceeds your income, your upkeep could be your downfall." A generation ago it was easier to live within one's means. When a person ran out of money, he simply didn't buy anything else. He was forced to budget or pay the price. But today we have so much easy credit available that we can overestimate our ability to pay for something and overspend our resources.

I constantly get credit card applications in the mail accompanied by a complimentary letter: "You are a *preferred* customer. Because of your outstanding credit rating, we are entrusting you with our maximum purchasing power." What hype! Proverbs 29:5 says, "Whoever flatters his neighbor is spreading a net for his feet." Researchers have proven that people will purchase 34 percent more with a credit card than with cash.[8] Don't you think the credit card companies know that?

Nevertheless, many of us get sucked in. We borrow the maximum allowed by the credit card company. When one account has reached its limit, we start another one, then a third. Soon we have fallen into the debt trap. The average American has a thirty-eight hundred dollar balance on his credit cards and is paying more than fifty dollars a month in interest. Credit card delinquency for the second quarter of 1996 was the worst in American history.[9] The average person's goal is to be able to afford what he's spending!

One of our local banks shared their research after reviewing applications for home loans:

- Ninety percent of all applicants had a minimum of four credit cards.
- Three of the four credit cards were at the maximum allowable limit.
- Eighty-two percent of the applicants had two car payments; the average payment was $326 for forty-eight months. (The average house payment in 1978 was only $300.)
- Seventy percent of all applicants showed some late payments on their credit reports.
- When faced with the decision to keep a new car or sell it in order to qualify for a home loan, 50 percent of young adult, first-time home buyers chose to keep the car and continue renting.
- Thirty-two percent of the young adults applying had overdrawn their checking account less than ninety days prior to the date of application.
- It would take an average of six years for each family to pay off their consumer debt—*if* they continued paying at current levels, stopped charging immediately, and added nothing to their credit balances.

The Book of Proverbs says, "In the house of the wise are stores of choice food and oil, but a foolish man devours all he has" (Proverbs 21:20).

The prodigal son realized he was in trouble. His spending had entrapped him. He was broke and hungry, and so were all his friends.

Fortunately the story doesn't end there for the prodigal son, and it doesn't have to end there for anyone else who has fallen into the debt trap. The prodigal did several things right to get himself out of the pigpen. The things he did were so simple that we can follow his example and find freedom for ourselves as well.

CHAPTER SEVEN

LESSONS LEARNED IN A PIGPEN

The rich rule over the poor,
and the borrower is servant to the lender.
PROVERBS 22:7

Getting in debt is as easy as getting down an ice-covered mountain.
Getting out of debt is just as difficult as climbing that same mountain.
RON BLUE

Gary Goodale had fallen into the debt trap. His creditors were pursuing him so intently that just opening his mailbox or hearing his phone ring made his stomach churn. He was twenty-six years old, making twelve hundred dollars a month, with over one hundred thousand dollars in debts. He had a house mortgage, two car payments, and eight credit cards, most with balances above their credit limits.

Gary says, "My marriage had deteriorated under the financial strain, and like most in these circumstances, it ended in divorce. The loss of my wife's income and the added burden of now maintaining two households brought me to the brink of financial ruin."

Gary decided to take responsibility for his actions. He sold his house and used the two thousand dollars' profit to move into a small, one-bedroom apartment. "I promised myself that I would never get into such a financial mess again and that I would do everything in my power to pay my debts," he said.

Gary completely changed his spending habits. Whatever wasn't an absolute necessity, he eliminated. He canceled newspaper and magazine subscriptions and cable television. He said no to any form of entertainment with a price tag (movies, sporting events, etc.). Before every purchase, he asked himself, "Do I really need this, or do I just want it?" He budgeted his groceries, drinking only water and cutting out all unnecessary food items. He put a classi-fied ad in the newspaper and sold the furniture and appliances he didn't need. His new habits gave him more free time, which he filled by reading everything he could find at the library on personal finances.

Almost immediately Gary had freed up about three hundred dollars a month to go toward debt retirement and savings. He began paying off the credit cards with the smallest balance. When one was eliminated, he moved to the next one. "Although my deci-sion to pay off credit cards with the smallest balance, instead of those charging the highest interest, may not have followed the most correct financial advice," he said, "paying off the smaller cards faster motivated me and so worked best for me."

Soon Gary had his spending under control and was begin-ning to crawl out of debt. He concluded, "Unquestionably, the changes I made in my lifestyle were an improvement, but they were not easy by any means. Lifestyle changes are the most diffi-cult changes you can make.... Until the changes are ingrained in your soul, there's always the temptation to fall back to your old ways. It took four years and a lot of desire, determination, self-discipline, self-sacrifice and perseverance,...but now I can say I am debt free. I also have an emergency cash fund large enough to manage almost any crisis, and I am currently saving and investing over 40 percent of my take-home pay." Gary says he still has to discipline himself to meet the financial goals he has set, and not all his financial problems disappeared with his debt. But the dif-ference, he says, "is that now I control my finances—they no longer control me."[1]

The prodigal son, like Gary, had exhausted his resources. He found himself penniless and alone. But the prodigal son, like Gary Goodale, took some right steps to get himself out of the trap into which he had fallen.

STEP 1: ACCEPT RESPONSIBILITY

[Jesus said,] "So [the prodigal son] went and hired himself out to a citizen of that country, who sent him to his fields to feed pigs." (Luke 15:15)

The prodigal got a job feeding pigs. It certainly wasn't a glamorous job, but it was a job. You have to commend him for that. He didn't demand that the government or some organization take care of him. He took the first step by accepting responsibility for his actions and his own welfare.

When a young man in our church suddenly found himself out of work just weeks before his marriage, he approached a wealthy friend of mine, Mike Cappy, for counsel. He said, "Mike, I don't want to make the wrong decision. What if I get into a job I don't like and then get stuck in it and can't take a better one? How do I know which job to take?"

Mike gave him some great advice that proved to be right on target. He said, "Son, find a job. It's easier to get a better job if you have a job already. People prefer to hire someone with a record of employment. Do well at that job, and if someone offers you a better job shortly thereafter, take it if you want. Your employer will understand. If he wants to pay you better for your services, he has that option."

The young man found a job quickly. He didn't like the job, and it paid much less than he was used to receiving, but he was able to enter marriage with dignity and self-confidence, knowing he would at least be supporting his new family. He said the fact that he disliked his job made him all the more ready to see his wife at the end of the day.

After several months the young man was offered a better-paying job in a vocation he enjoyed. If he hadn't taken Mike's advice, he might have been out of work for nearly a year. Instead, he says the lessons he learned were invaluable. He learned to work hard even when he didn't feel like it, he gained an appreciation for his new bride, and he now sympathizes with people who spend much of their lives in jobs they don't enjoy. Today he often shares the advice he got from Mike with other young men who find themselves out of work.

When we find ourselves headed for the debt trap, it's tempting to look for a quick fix like a lottery ticket or a get-rich-quick scheme. Those things, however, will only get us into more trouble. The only true, long-range solution is to be disciplined and willing to do the difficult things to break our habits and get out of the traps we're in.

It may be necessary to work at a meager job. We may not see a way out, and the numbers may not add up, but God honors those who work, and he will reward our efforts. Proverbs 10:4 reads, "Lazy hands make a man poor, but diligent hands bring wealth." Not only will God reward us, but our self-esteem will return as we take responsibility for our own actions.

STEP 2: ACKNOWLEDGE THE BONDAGE

[Jesus said,] "When he came to his senses, he said, 'How many of my father's hired men have food to spare, and here I am starving to death!'" (Luke 15:17)

The prodigal realized he was worse off than the servants of his father because he had become a slave to his past mistakes. He was used to total independence. Now he was completely dependent on a pig farmer.

When a person goes deeply in debt, he becomes a servant. He no longer works for himself. He is not free to do whatever he wants with his income. He cannot invest in what he wants, spend on what he wants, or give away as much as he wishes, because he is a servant to the lender, usually a credit card company or the local bank. The lender gets a certain amount of his income, and he has no choice in the matter, unless he steals what rightfully belongs to the lender by not paying his bills.

You've probably seen that bumper sticker that reads, "I owe, I owe, so it's off to work I go." Most Americans have enslaved themselves to a creditor, and they know they must go to work, not for their own benefit, but to pay off their debts.

In any addiction, one of the first steps toward getting well is to admit we are sick; one of the first steps toward freedom is admitting we are in bondage. Proverbs 27:12 says, "The prudent see danger and take refuge, but the simple keep going and suffer for it."

How would you rate your level of financial freedom? Check yourself against the following ten indicators of financial bondage. If two to four of these apply to you, be on guard and change some habits so you don't fall into the debt trap. If five to seven apply, it's time to make dramatic changes in your life to get out of the trap you've fallen into. If eight or more apply to you, then you are in financial bondage, and it would be wise for you immediately to seek the advice of a Christian financial counselor.

Ten Indicators of Financial Bondage

- *Guilt.* Every time you go out to eat, buy a child a present, or spend money on entertainment, you feel guilty because you're thinking the money should go to pay off debts. Even though you know you should read this book, you dread it!
- *Deception.* When you go out with others, you feel hypocritical; it seems you are always pretending to live on a level that's not real.
- *Stress.* You find yourself stalling creditors (80 percent of American families experience the pressure of overdue bills).
- *Preoccupation.* You are so worried about money matters that you find it difficult to think about and enjoy other things.

- *Bickering.* "Money" is a fighting word in your home. The subject is a frequent source of contention and hassle.
- *Envy.* You are jealous of others who have more.
- *Resentment.* You are angry at God for not increasing your supply.
- *Loneliness.* You feel alienated from friends who appear free of financial pressures, and you are uncomfortable in church because you can't give what you know you should. No one knows but you.
- *Hopelessness.* You are getting deeper and deeper into debt and see no way out. Or for the past five years you have said, "I think we will be in good shape in two more years."
- *Low Self-esteem.* You feel like a failure as you move farther away from the image you project and the financial freedom you want to experience.

How would you score yourself? Do you have a debt problem you need to humbly admit to God? God's grace is sufficient. He can forgive whatever decisions or actions might have caused you to stumble into this trap. And he will provide a way out. He will set you free, but he first wants you to admit you are in bondage.

Let me add a word of caution here about these ten indicators. It's possible to spend an extraordinary proportion of our income on interest and debt retirement without having any of these reactions. If we make enough money to pay off our monthly credit bills without much sacrifice, we can spend hundreds or thousands of additional dollars on items purchased on credit and never feel guilty or have any financial trouble. Even though we may avoid being enslaved by debt because of a large income, this is still poor stewardship. If we're paying a high interest rate on debts we've incurred to buy nonessential items like boats and sports cars, or nicer clothes than necessary, or extravagant vacations, then we need to reevaluate our spending habits and ask ourselves if we're using the money God has given us as wisely as possible. I'm not saying it's wrong to purchase these things, but there is a time to do so and a way to do so that honors God, which we will discuss later.

STEP 3: DEVELOP A PLAN

[The son said,] "I will set out and go back to my father and say to him: Father, I have sinned against heaven and against you. I am no longer worthy to be called your son; make me like one of your hired men." (Luke 15:18–19)

If we want to escape financial bondage, we need a plan. We can't go on living as we have been and somehow wish our way out of debt. Jesus said, "A man building a tower should first sit down and calculate the cost, lest he have to quit halfway through and be the laughingstock of the community" (Luke 14:28–30, my paraphrase).

Some people think they will get out of debt simply by refusing to spend any money they don't have to spend. But it doesn't work. Each month we're faced with difficult priority decisions, and the lines between "wants" and "needs" can be unclear. If we determine to spend only what is absolutely necessary, we leave ourselves no breathing room. We feel miserable being so confined, until finally we give in and spend money on something we really don't need. Then we feel guilty for not doing everything possible to get out of debt, and the process begins again. It becomes a difficult cycle to break.

In order to release ourselves from bondage, we need a specific plan, a list of realistic steps we can take to climb out of debt. Proverbs 21:5 says, "The plans of the diligent lead to profit as surely as haste leads to poverty." One step is surely to budget our income, which we will discuss in greater detail in the next chapter. We may need to cut up our credit cards, sell our house and move to a smaller one, trade in our car for an older model, cut out costly entertainment, or discipline our eating habits. We may, in fact, need to do all of the above.

If you find yourself caught in the debt trap, write down your plan and discuss it with your family. Ask someone to hold you accountable, perhaps even someone outside your family. Begin praying that God will reward your plan and give you the discipline to stick to it.

STEP 4: SUBMIT TO THE FATHER'S WILL

[The son said,] "I will...say to him: Father, I have sinned against heaven and against you. I am no longer worthy to be called your son; make me like one of your hired men." (Luke 15:18–19)

When we start down the wrong path, usually there are warnings. A friend may express concern. A sermon may make us feel guilty. We might find ourselves hiding the truth or arguing with our spouse or parents about the same subject over and over.

Sometimes our refusal to heed the warnings is based on our pride. Nobody likes to take advice from someone else or realize he has been wrong. The prodigal admitted he was not as smart as he thought and that his foolish pride had gotten him into trouble. He began to demonstrate a submissive, teachable spirit, perhaps for the first time in years. As a result, he set out for home, determined to humble himself before his father and ask for his forgiveness. Likewise, when we find ourselves in financial trouble, we need to humble ourselves before our Father and ask for forgiveness and guidance.

STEP 5: START IMMEDIATELY

[Jesus said,] "So he got up and went to his father." (Luke 15:20)

The prodigal son didn't wait long enough to change his mind. Once he resolved to fix his problem and devised his plan, he immediately put it into action.

He did have one advantage over many people in debt: He was single. He had no one to blame but himself, and he didn't have to convince anyone else to agree to his plan.

One caution to you who are married: Your financial plan should not be allowed to cause a division between you and your spouse. It's so easy for husbands and wives to accuse each other and bicker over financial problems. Don't fight with your spouse over this issue. A marriage is more important than a plan to get out of debt, but your marriage will be much healthier if you can agree on a plan to free you from debt. Start the discussion today. In love, sit down together, communicate about your situation, and come to a compromise solution.

But start immediately! Although it may take a long time to recover fully, you will feel better just knowing you are beginning to get things under control.

THE FATHER'S RESPONSE

The prodigal son had a long, exhausting trip home—plenty of time to second-guess himself hundreds of times. "My father will never take me back. I've wounded him too deeply. I've been a disgrace to my family, but I must try. If I don't go, I'll always wonder what might have happened. He's a gracious man. Maybe he will find it in his heart to forgive me."

> "But while he was still a long way off, his father saw him and was filled with compassion for him; he ran to his son, threw his arms around him and kissed him.
>
> "The son said to him, 'Father, I have sinned against heaven and against you. I am no longer worthy to be called your son.'
>
> "But the father said to his servants, 'Quick! Bring

the best robe and put it on him. Put a ring on his finger and sandals on his feet. Bring the fattened calf and kill it. Let's have a feast and celebrate. For this son of mine was dead and is alive again; he was lost and is found.' So they began to celebrate." (Luke 15:20–24)

Instead of hearing the lecture he expected, the son was greeted by an enthusiastic and loving father who embraced him, muffled his repentant cry in his chest, and restored him immediately to sonship. Then the father threw a party! This scrawny, hollow-cheeked, disheveled boy who had wasted his father's hard-earned money was robed and crowned and treated like a king.

I believe God will do that for you and me. When we come to God and admit humbly that we have been poor stewards of his money and have allowed ourselves to fall into indulgence, wasteful spending, and debt, the Father still embraces us, offers his grace and forgiveness, and restores us as his children. He even allows us to partake again in the riches of his kingdom.

If you have fallen into the debt trap, why not come before God today and humbly accept responsibility for your actions? Don't trivialize the situation. Have the character to determine you will pay back those to whom you are indebted. Admit you've spent more than your resources allowed. Acknowledge your bondage, develop a plan, and then submit to the will of the Father. He will forgive you, and he will help you to discipline your spending, pay back your creditors, and escape the debt trap.

> The LORD is compassionate and gracious,
>   slow to anger, abounding in love.
> He will not always accuse,
>   nor will he harbor his anger forever;
> he does not treat us as our sins deserve
>   or repay us according to our iniquities.

For as high as the heavens are above the earth,
    so great is his love for those who fear him;
as far as the east is from the west,
    so far has he removed our transgressions from us.
As a father has compassion on his children,
    so the LORD has compassion on those who fear him;
for he knows how we are formed,
    he remembers that we are dust.
As for man, his days are like grass,
    he flourishes like a flower of the field;
the wind blows over it and it is gone,
    and its place remembers it no more.
But from everlasting to everlasting
    the LORD's love is with those who fear him,
    and his righteousness with their children's children—
with those who keep his covenant
    and remember to obey his precepts.

(Psalm 103:8–18)

CHAPTER EIGHT

THE KEYS TO WISE SPENDING

Be sure you know the condition of your flocks,
give careful attention to your herds;
for riches do not endure forever,
and a crown is not secure for all generations.
PROVERBS 27:23–24

Budgeting is the thing to do. / On that I'm most emphatic.
I'm just as broke as I ever was, / But now it's systematic!
ANONYMOUS

One day as a large crowd was traveling along with Jesus, he began to teach them about commitment and about counting the cost. He said, "Suppose one of you wants to build a tower. Will he not first sit down and estimate the cost to see if he has enough money to complete it? For if he lays the foundation and is not able to finish it, everyone who sees it will ridicule him, saying, 'This fellow began to build and was not able to finish'" (Luke 14:28–30).

Whenever I read Jesus' words about building a tower, I think about a half-built castle that can be seen in the countryside between Louisville and Lexington, Kentucky. Several years ago the huge walls and towers for a medieval-looking castle were built, evidently by a man whose wife was in love with castles. He ran out of money before he could finish it. So out in the middle of nowhere, on Versailles Road in Kentucky, you can drive by the walls and towers, but there is no castle! Over the years it has drawn a lot of attention, and as you can imagine, ridicule.

As I write this, our church is in the process of relocating. In our current location, we are trying to cram ten thousand people into a building designed for twenty-five hundred. We have five weekend services, and our parking lot is a mess. We knew if we were to continue reaching out to those who do not know Christ, something had to change. The congregation decided to build a new facility. Therefore, we're building a multimillion-dollar facility on nearly one hundred acres of land.

Even to begin such a huge endeavor has required a tremendous step of faith. If God were not in this building project, we would fail miserably. But it would be foolish of us, and poor stewardship, if we didn't also have detailed plans for not only how we are going to build the building but how we will pay for it. As Jesus alluded, God expects the church to have faith but also to use common sense and wise planning in allocating the resources he has given us.

The same is true in the personal life of every believer. Though we are to live by faith, trusting God to take care of us, we are also to manage our money wisely so we can provide for our families and give generously to others.

BEGIN WITH A BUDGET

The best way to manage our money and stay out of debt is to develop a disciplined spending plan—a budget that allocates a certain amount of money each month to categories of spending or saving. When my wife and I were first married, I made seventy dollars a week as a preacher, and she made sixty-five dollars as a teletype operator in a brokerage firm. After tithing and paying our taxes, we had to live on about one hundred dollars a week. Our budget was simple. We kept seven envelopes in a drawer, each labeled for either tithe, housing, food, gasoline, utilities, auto, or miscellaneous. If someone said, "Come with us to the Reds' game," and we only had four dollars in the miscellaneous envelope, we told them we couldn't go. We did our best not to dip into an envelope for any reason other than the intended expenditures.

For most people, a budget is an envelope system without the

envelopes. It can be done on paper or with a computer software program. (However, if someone is really struggling with his money, the envelope system is the simplest budgeting technique, and it still works!) A budget is like a road map that guides us and tells us when we are on course. Just like not having a map in a strange city creates anxiety, frustration, and fear, so does operating without a budget.

Most people think financial freedom will come when they get a 10 percent raise. But the Bible says, "He who *ignores discipline* comes to poverty and shame" (Proverbs 13:18, emphasis added). The key is not more money, but a disciplined, well-planned spending budget. I know people making eighteen thousand dollars a year who are debt free. Yet everyone has heard of athletes or entertainers making millions of dollars who have declared bankruptcy. It has little to do with how much we make, and everything to do with how much we spend. Budgeting won't ensure prosperity, but it will keep us from overspending our resources and will help us avoid the debt trap.

I know it's more difficult for some people to budget than others. If you're a salesman living off a commission or if you're self-employed, it's impossible to know what your exact income will be. But you can make a conservative estimate and live accordingly. Proverbs 14:15 says, "A simple man believes anything, but a prudent man gives thought to his steps."

However, although most of us understand the need for a good budget, few of us really follow through. Only 25 percent of American families operate on a budget. Fifty percent say they want to budget but never get around to it. Some people even claim they make more than they need anyway and can get along fine without a budget, but a good plan will help anyone be a better steward of his resources.

Determine that you will be more disciplined than most. Make a plan and stick to it. Here's a way to get started.

PRIORITIZE YOUR EXPENDITURES

When you're planning your budget, prioritize your expenditures first. Make a list of what is most important to you. Richard Case, author of *The Money Diet,* suggests that we go through our checkbooks and make a list of all expenditures, placing each in one of three columns: (1) must have, (2) should have, and (3) like to have. He explains: "'Must haves' include such things as housing, food, shelter, automobile, utilities, insurance, and taxes. 'Should haves' include such things as clothes, furniture, etc. All the rest are 'like to haves.'"[1]

When you create a list of priorities, it's important to involve your family so everyone understands the priorities and is focused on the goals. Explain to your mate and your children exactly where you are financially and what you're doing. Author Randy Alcorn suggests that we teach our children to budget by bringing home one paycheck in all tens or all ones and dividing up the bills on the kitchen counter according to the budget categories. Then the children can begin to visualize how much money it takes to buy a home and a car, pay the electric bill, and buy groceries. Maybe the next time you ask your kids to turn off the lights as you're leaving the house, they'll understand why.[2]

As you're developing a budget with your family, consider the following six priorities.

PRIORITY 1: PAY THE LORD FIRST

I once heard Bob Benson, a beloved Christian author, talk about a vest he had worn to a speaking engagement. He was very concerned about his message and wanted to make a good impression, but when he got home, he realized his vest had been buttoned wrong. It had been cockeyed during his entire speech. He was humiliated. "You know, it is so easy to button your vest wrong," he later said. "You only have to get the first button wrong, and then all the others follow suit."

The same is true with our priorities. If we get the first one wrong, all the others are going to be out of place. But if we get this first priority right, each step thereafter is much easier. At the top of our lists should be our planned giving to the church. God makes it clear he is to receive the firstfruits of our income, not the left-overs: "Honor the LORD with your wealth, with the *firstfruits* of all your crops" (Proverbs 3:9, emphasis added).

How much of our income is to be given to God as the firstfruits? Although we will discuss the tithing principle and other ways to give the Lord our "firstfruits" in more detail later, let me say that my personal conviction is that I should give the first 10 percent of my income to my local church. Whatever your conviction, decide to give God what you consider to be the "firstfruits" of your income, to show God you understand it's not your money you're managing, but his.

We're tempted to think that if we give God 10 percent, then we're giving him his part. After that, once we pay our bills, we're free to do whatever we wish with the remainder. But God is not concerned with only the first 10 percent. Just as we can't say, "I went to church on Sunday and I've done my part; now I may live as I wish," neither can we claim the right to do what we want with the remaining 90 percent of our income. God owns all of it and cares how we manage it all.

The key to honoring God with our finances is remembering that our money is really not our money. Psalm 24:1 says, "The earth is the LORD's, and everything in it." God owns it all and gives to us as he pleases. No matter how much we like to think we earned it, we don't have anything that God didn't give us. The first job Adam and Eve were given—even before they fell into sin—was management. They were put in charge of the Garden of Eden. They were to tend it, but they did not own it. In the same way, we are only tending what is in our possession. Nothing we have will be ours for eternity. Whatever we have came from God and will return to God.

In the meantime we are to be stewards—managers or trustees—of God's resources, and God takes a steward's task seriously. The Bible has more than two thousand verses on money and possessions, exhorting us to be wise stewards of God's resources. Some day he will demand an accounting of that which he has entrusted to us. The Bible says, "It is required that those who have been given a trust must prove faithful" (1 Corinthians 4:2). God has entrusted us with quite a lot of his resources. If you average an annual income of twenty-five thousand dollars over a forty-year period, you will manage more than a million dollars in your lifetime!

PRIORITY 2: PAY BILLS ON TIME

Paul instructs us, *"Give everyone what you owe him: If you owe taxes, pay taxes; if revenue, then revenue; if respect, then respect; if honor, then honor"* (Romans 13:7, emphasis added). We are to pay what we owe.

Establish a budget that allows you to pay all your bills in full and on time each month. If you can't pay them all, pay something on all of them and communicate your intentions of paying everything to those you owe. If possible, pay in full at least those bills that accumulate each month—the mortgage, utilities, etc. If you can't do even that, it's time to sell your house and move to a smaller one, or sell your car and drive an older model, or make some drastic cuts until your outgo matches your income. If you're having trouble even putting food on the table, work as hard as you can (at the most menial jobs if necessary), pray that the Lord will take care of you, and seek financial advice from a Christian counselor.

If you're married, decide which spouse has the better financial skills to assure the bills get paid on time and proper records are kept. Sometimes it's the husband; in other cases the wife is more detail-oriented and adept at keeping good financial records. This shouldn't spark an argument about who will maintain control, but it should be an open dialogue, with the most capable person willingly taking the job as a servant, not a dictator. A husband shouldn't be too proud to let his wife handle the checkbook if she is gifted in that area.

Wayne Smith, a well-known preacher-friend of mine in Kentucky, said that when he and his wife were first married forty years ago he bought a bus, thinking it was a good investment. When he lost money on the bus, his wife asked if she could take over the finances. Marge has run the checkbook ever since, giving Wayne a monthly allowance that he may spend as he pleases. He says he never has a financial problem (he doesn't have the opportunity), and the bills are always paid on time. Both partners know how the money is spent, but Wayne has been sharp enough and humble enough to take advantage of his wife's skills.

PRIORITY 3: GET OUT OF DEBT AS SOON AS POSSIBLE

Though some Christians preach that we shouldn't be in debt to anyone, the Bible doesn't prohibit debt altogether. Deuteronomy 15:8 commands us to lend freely to the poor. If lending money is not wrong, borrowing money cannot be wrong. God wouldn't command us to do something that would cause someone else to behave improperly. What God does say, through Paul, is, *"Let no debt remain outstanding,* except the continuing debt to love one another, for he who loves his fellowman has fulfilled the law" (Romans 13:8, emphasis added).

At times acquiring a low-interest loan can even prove to be wise stewardship if, for instance, the money is invested in a home that appreciates in value or in a well-organized and financially profitable business. But debt carries with it heavy responsibilities. Allowing ourselves to become slaves to creditors is unwise behavior and poor stewardship.

Before Assuming More Debt...

If you're considering applying for a loan or purchasing something on credit, first ask a trusted financial counselor if the loan makes good financial sense. Then, before acquiring more debt of any kind, ask yourself three questions. If the answer to any of them is yes, don't take on another loan.

Am I so deep in debt that I can't pay my bills on time? I know some Christians who have so much debt they're depending on the rapture of Christ to get them out! That is dishonest and irresponsible. We should "let no debt remain outstanding." To become so enslaved in debt that we cannot pay our bills is not only bad stewardship, it is breaking the promise we made to those who loaned us the money.

Am I abusing my credit card privilege? For most of us, our problem with debt is tied to credit cards. Just as a person on a diet may have to throw out the chocolate chip cookies, some of us need to cut up our credit cards and refuse to use them altogether.

There is nothing inherently evil about credit cards. In fact, they can be a valuable asset in establishing a positive credit record so we can borrow money for an investment, like a house. If you don't charge more than you have the resources to pay back, and if you are able to pay off your credit card bills at the end of each month, then perhaps you are using credit cards to your advantage. If so, you are a rare person.

The banking industry bets that you won't be disciplined enough to pay off your credit card debts every month. If everyone did, they wouldn't make any money. In fact, some banking circles refer to people who pay off their debts each month as "deadbeats." A deadbeat used to be someone who didn't pay his bills. Now it's someone who pays so well he doesn't allow the bank to make any money.

Here are the most common ways we misuse credit cards:

- Buying luxuries or nonessentials with credit cards. (Paying for vacations, entertainment, clothes, jewelry, or eating out on credit must be avoided.)
- Paying the minimum amount due, rather than the entire bill, at the end of the month. (Failing to pay off the credit card bill in full each month is the most common first step toward the debt trap.)
- Assuming that if we have the credit to buy it, we can afford it. (This is far from the truth.)
- Accepting a new credit card without paying off the old. (Transferring the credit card balance to a card with a lower interest rate is wise, but make sure you cancel your old card.)
- Using a credit card to purchase things that would normally be purchased with cash. (Buying groceries on credit, for instance, is a sign that you are falling into the debt trap.)

Walter Cavanaugh is the most avid credit card collector in the country. Cavanaugh, a pharmacist, claims to own 1,199 valid credit cards! "Mr. Plastic Fantastic," as he's known, collects them for fun and stores all but a few of them in a safe-deposit box. He estimates that if he used his 800 credit cards, he would have a credit line approaching $1.4 million![3] Before you get any ideas, what do you think would happen if he went on a sudden spending spree? He would be rich for thirty days, then a slave or a fugitive for the rest of his life as he tried to pay back or run from his creditors.

Bottom line? Just because a bank or credit card company grants a line of credit, don't think you can afford to use it.

Am I beginning a debt habit? Let's say you want new family room furniture. The old sofa is really out-of-date and threadbare, or the room is empty and you're embarrassed. My wife and I lived for two years with lawn chairs in our family room until we could afford new furniture, but maybe you're a little self-conscious and can't bring yourself to do that. You decide you need the furniture now, so you spend $5,000 to redecorate the room, which you put on a credit card at 18 percent interest. You start paying it back, making $127-a-month payments for five years. So that furniture eventually costs you $7,620.

That's bad enough, but even worse is the pattern you have established. About the time the furniture is paid off, you need a new playground set for the kids in the backyard. It can't wait; they're growing up too fast. You also need a video camera for pictures. So you continue using your credit card, paying nearly double for everything and getting yourself deeper and deeper into debt. As someone said, "It's tough to plan for the future when you're too busy fixing the things you did yesterday."

When you're planning a budget, set a goal to get completely out of debt as soon as possible, perhaps with the exception of your home mortgage. It doesn't make sense to put money each month into a savings account earning 3 percent interest if you owe several thousand dollars on your credit cards at 18 percent interest or have a car loan at 8 percent interest.

The Steps to Getting Out of Debt

Pay off the credit cards first. Ask your card issuers to lower your interest rate. With the competition in the market, they may be willing. Then start paying off the cards with the highest interest rate. Consider paying off your credit cards by taking money from savings—if you're earning 3 or 4 percent in savings and paying 18 percent on your credit cards.

Determine you won't use a credit card unless you have the money to pay the bill in its entirety at the end of the month. Instead of buying things on credit, develop the habit of saving for any nonessential item and then paying for it in cash. It might mean living with lawn chairs in the family room, going without a kitchen table and eating on the floor for a couple of months, or doing without a dishwasher or a television for a while. But refusing to buy those things on credit will put you in better financial condition, teach you self-discipline, and give you a sense of contentment with the simple blessings God has given. You might even have some great memories of the times you truly did without!

Once an automobile is paid off, don't trade it in. Financial experts agree that the cheapest car you can buy is the one you already own, and you should plan to drive your car for ten years. When your car is paid off, begin saving for the next automobile, and make it your goal to pay for it in cash.

Pay extra principle on your home mortgage. You can pay off your home mortgage in much less time and save thousands of dollars if you will pay more than required each month. For instance, suppose you have a thirty-year loan at eight percent on a $100,000 home. If you will pay an extra $102.68 each month, you will pay for your home in twenty years. Not only will you be debt free, but you will have saved $63,407 in interest payments. For more information, I recommend a book by Marc Eisenson called *A Banker's Secret,* published by Good Advice Press.[4]

Develop sales resistance. While you're working to pay off your debts, you must discipline yourself against spending more than necessary for items you don't need.

I heard about a salesman who assured a female shopper, "Ma'am, you can save enough on your food bill to pay for this new microwave."

The woman replied, "We're already paying for a washing machine with the laundry bills we're saving, and a new car with the bus fare we're saving. I just don't see how we can afford to save any more money right now!"

It has been said, "The pain of the payment always exceeds the pleasure of the purchase." The most practical advice about budgeting is simply this: Live within your means. Don't spend more than you make. You will be happier living in a $50,000 house with easy payments than a $200,000 house with stress. You'll be happier doing without a VCR and cable television than wondering how you can pay the bills. If you learn to say no to some things, I promise you will be more content than if you had indulged in everything your heart desired.

PRIORITY 4: PLAN FOR EMERGENCIES

The prodigal son got in trouble because he didn't anticipate the famine. We can't predict every famine in our lives, and we must trust the Lord to take care of us in difficult times. But we also have to be wise enough to realize that small emergencies can eat at our budget every month.

- The dog gets sick and costs you seventy-five dollars in veterinarian bills.
- Your car's radiator dies, resulting in a three-hundred-dollar repair.
- Your in-laws decide to come for a couple of days, and you need an extra fifty dollars for groceries.
- It's back-to-school time. You have to pay for new clothes and supplies and library fees. Suddenly you're out two or three hundred dollars, or maybe a lot more.
- Your cousin's getting married, and you don't dare show up at the wedding without a gift. You have to find at least twenty-five dollars for a respectable wedding present.

We could think of hundreds of little emergencies that crop up each month that cost more than our budget anticipated. Then there are the annual extra expenses, like insurance bills, Christmas gifts, auto licenses, and doctor visits. We need to allow for each of these in our monthly budgets.

One thing that really hurt me early in my adult life was high taxes. Ministers are usually considered self-employed, which means taxes are not extracted from our paychecks and we must pay the entire Social Security burden. At first I paid my taxes annually, attempting to save and invest throughout the year in preparation for April 15. But I almost always underestimated the bill. Then Social Security taxes escalated rapidly. I found myself borrowing to pay taxes, working all year to pay off the loan, then borrowing again the next year to pay them off again. It was an endless cycle, and one that tended to get worse and worse. It took me years to discipline myself to plan ahead sufficiently.

Don't make that same mistake. Study your checkbook, and determine how much you spent last year on things that don't fit into your monthly budget categories. Set aside a miscellaneous fund to cover as much of those expenses as possible.

PRIORITY 5: USE SOME RESOURCES FOR PERSONAL ENJOYMENT

A lot of Christians get out of balance when they realize whose money they are managing. They begin to feel guilty if they spend any on themselves or their own families. They think all the money should be saved for the future or given to the poor and none should be spent just on fun. But I believe our heavenly Father gives us some of his resources for our pleasure. As 1 Timothy 6:17 says, "Command those who are rich in this present world not to be arrogant nor to put their hope in wealth, which is so uncertain, but to put their hope in God, who richly provides us with everything *for our enjoyment*" (emphasis added).

A couple of years ago I had four extra tickets to a basketball game between the University of Louisville and the University of Kentucky. In Kentucky, college basketball is almost a religion, and to attend such an event is a rare opportunity. I gave the tickets to my sons and their wives, who were ecstatic about going because they are avid basketball fans. They could have sold the tickets for hundreds of dollars and put the money in the bank for my grandchildren's education, but I didn't want them to. I wanted them to have fun. When I looked across the arena and saw them enjoying themselves, I was pleased because I love them. (It was a good thing I had enough tickets for all of us because I'm only so generous!)

God loves us as a father loves his children. He is pleased when we are good stewards and are generous with what he has given us, but I believe he also loves to see us enjoying his blessings. After we have managed our money wisely and given generously, there comes a time for us to enjoy the fruits of our labor. Tony Campolo calls it "party time." He points out that the Levites were instructed to take the tithe that had been brought to the tabernacle and use it to throw a big feast every year for the Israelites to enjoy (see Deuteronomy 14:22–27).[5]

Are you paying your bills on time? Are you giving generously? Are you saving some for the future? Are you doing all these things and still demanding that your family pinch every penny? Then maybe it's time for you to lighten up and throw a party! If you're doing your best to honor God with your money, don't feel guilty about spending some to take a vacation, eat out, entertain guests, or take your family to a ball game.

I think Campolo's "10 percent party rule" (my terminology) is a good one. Look at the things on your "like to have" list. If you're spending more than 10 percent of your monthly income on cable television, eating out, hobbies, entertainment, or other items on your "like to have" list, that may reveal some areas where you should cut back. If you're taking care of all your other priorities and are spending 10 percent or less on yourself, then don't feel guilty. Allow yourself to enjoy the fruits of your labor. Keep a balance between wise stewardship and wise spending, and remember that God is a loving heavenly Father who is gratified when you are able to enjoy the fruits of his blessings.

PRIORITY 6: INVEST THE REMAINDER WISELY

In chapter one, we discussed the parable of the talents, a story Jesus told about a man who gave three servants different sums of money to invest for him while he was gone. One of the servants buried his money in a field instead of investing it. When the master returned, he said to the servant, "You wicked, lazy servant! So you knew that I harvest where I have not sown and gather where I have not scattered seed? Well then, you should have put my money on deposit with the bankers, so that when I returned I would have received it back with interest" (Matthew 25:26–27).

It's wasteful to sit on our money and do nothing. The very least we can do is put it in the bank where it can earn the minimum amount of interest. The best we can do is make wise, long-term investments that could substantially increase our money in a few years.

Take Advantage of Compound Interest

If you place ten thousand dollars in the bank at 3 percent interest, in twenty years it will be worth eighteen thousand dollars. If that same ten thousand dollars were invested in a mutual fund, earning just 6 percent (which would be a poor return for a mutual fund), in twenty years your money would be worth thirty-two thousand dollars. If you were able to get a 10 percent return on your investment through mutual funds, stocks, or other wise investments, in twenty years your original ten thousand dollars would be sixty-seven thousand dollars!

Let's suppose a young man named Jack has a paper route, beginning in the second grade. He puts six hundred dollars a year in an Individual Retirement Account until he graduates from high school. Though he never makes other investments, he doesn't touch the money until he turns sixty-five.

A young woman named Jill, who is the same age as Jack, becomes a lawyer. At age twenty-five, she begins putting two thousand dollars a year in an IRA and continues to do so every year till she turns sixty-five.

When they turn sixty-five, both Jack and Jill will be millionaires, but Jack will actually be richer than Jill. Yet he will have invested a total of sixty-six hundred dollars while she invested eighty thousand dollars![6]

The principle of compound interest is so incredible it has been called the eighth wonder of the world. As Americans we are blessed by God to live in a nation that has enjoyed prosperity and economic stability. We can be fairly confident we will receive a good return on our money if we invest wisely. Although investing always involves risk, Jesus commended the servants who risked their money wisely as "good and faithful," while referring to the one living in fear as "lazy." That parable should free us to feel confident about taking risks and doing our best to invest wisely the resources God has given us.

Beware of High-Risk Investments

I believe God will honor wise investments, made out of a sincere desire to be good stewards of what he has given us. But when a person promises we will get rich quick if we invest in his product or company, that should be a warning. Wise investors know there is no such thing as a free lunch. Some of the silliest and most wasteful purchases we can make are "investments" in get-rich-quick schemes and high-risk stocks. They're often little more than gambling. Proverbs 13:11 says, "Dishonest money dwindles away, but he who gathers money little by little makes it grow."

Sometimes people have difficulty determining whether something is an investment or just gambling. When does investing become gambling? I believe that buying stocks in successful companies, for example, can be a wise investment. To loan a company money and get a return on my investment is a benefit to both me and that company. No one has to lose money in order for me to gain. If I choose a company that has a good track record, has provided a good service to the community, and is led by people of character, then I believe I have made a wise investment without undue risk.

The master in Jesus' parable said the lazy servant at least should have put the money in the bank so it could have gained interest. It seems the master felt that saving the money in the bank was the least that should have been done. Today, with the popularity of mutual funds, even a beginning investor can diversify quickly by investing in a mutual fund. The risk is not too great, and the return is good.

But there are thousands of investing options, some of which are very risky. Whenever you're trying to determine if an investment might cross the line into gambling, ask yourself two questions.

Are the chances good that I will lose money in this investment? Ask your financial adviser what percentage of people lose money in such an investment. For example, 90 percent of those who trade in futures and stock options lose money.[7] If it's likely you'll lose money, it can't be a wise investment.

Must others lose money in order for me to gain money in this investment? In gambling—on sports activities, in the lottery, in slot machines and card games—you only win when someone else loses. Many forms of stock options and trading in futures fit this category as well. While people may purchase certain options as a kind of insurance policy to protect their investment, many people buy futures and stock options because they're betting on what is going to happen to the market. They may not realize it, but they are betting against someone else who has the opposite opinion about the future of the market. For them to win, their opponents must lose. Such activity is a lot like gambling and is quite different from purchasing a piece or stock of a company that you think will perform its service well.

Though the Bible doesn't say, "Thou shalt not gamble," to do so is not wise stewardship. As I mentioned earlier, it cannot befit a Christian's character to gain money for doing nothing, and at someone else's expense.

But there is still a gray area. Many legitimate investments have higher risks than others and yet may prove to be wise purchases under the right circumstances. Check your priorities. Paul wrote to Timothy, "People who want to get rich fall into temptation and a trap and into many foolish and harmful desires that plunge men into ruin and destruction. For the love of money is a root of all kinds of evil" (1 Timothy 6:9–10). Beware of the trap of wanting to get rich quick. Ask yourself if your motive is to invest your money to make it grow, or to gamble it in hopes of making a quick profit with little effort.

Financial counselor Austin Pryor offers the following cardinal rules about selecting an investment:

- Choose an investment consistent with a specific, biblically sound, long-term strategy.
- Choose an investment only after you have prayed about it and considered trusted, experienced Christian counsel.
- Choose an investment you understand.
- Choose an investment that makes common sense.
- Choose an investment that fits comfortably with your temperament.[8]

One last caution. While following biblical guidelines for handling money and staying out of debt is critical, we can be perfect money managers and still fail miserably in honoring God with our money. God cares even more about our hearts. We can get our spending under control, give a tithe to the church, save wisely, and still fall into one of the traps mentioned earlier—the success trap or the comparison trap. In fact, we might be more likely to fall into them if we are managing our money well.

When it comes to our money, a balance must be maintained, a balance between trust and planning. Jesus taught us not to worry about tomorrow. He promised that if God provides for the birds of the air and the lilies of the field, he will surely take care of us. But he also encouraged us to plan ahead diligently (Luke 14:28–30). Our trust in God's providence should be balanced with a wise attention to financial details.

PART 3

■

AVOIDING THE SAVINGS TRAP

CHAPTER NINE

CAN YOU SAVE TOO MUCH?

*A man who has riches without understanding
is like the beasts that perish.*
PSALM 49:20

What to get the man who has everything—a burglar alarm.
ADVERTISEMENT FOR A SECURITY SYSTEM

Hetty Green lived in a shack. She ate cold oatmeal because heating it up would increase the electric bill. When her son injured his leg, she searched so long for a clinic offering free medical treatment that gangrene set in, and his leg had to be amputated. But when Henrietta Howland Green died in 1916, she was not poor. She had an estate worth more than ninety-five million dollars! One bank account alone had more than thirty-one million dollars in it![1]

Is it possible to be too frugal? You bet. Is it possible to save too much money? Absolutely. Jesus told of a rich man who hoarded his money and was condemned by God for his greed.

> And he told them this parable: "The ground of a certain rich man produced a good crop. He thought to himself, 'What shall I do? I have no place to store my crops.'
>
> "Then he said, 'This is what I'll do. I will tear down my barns and build bigger ones, and there I will store all my grain and my goods. And I'll say to myself, "You have plenty of good things laid up for many years. Take life easy; eat, drink and be merry."'
>
> "But God said to him, 'You fool! This very night

your life will be demanded from you. Then who will get what you have prepared for yourself?'

"This is how it will be with anyone who stores up things for himself but is not rich toward God." (Luke 12:16–21)

That man is the patron saint of the businessman of the 1990s. He thought only of the bottom line. *How can I provide for my future security? What is the ultimate investment?* The world would label him as a shrewd and wise investor. But God called him a fool.

YOU MAY BE FALLING INTO THE SAVINGS TRAP IF...

Most of us wouldn't consider ourselves hoarders. We're just "smart" with our money or "frugal;" we "know the value of a dollar." If you're wondering whether this chapter applies to you, here are some signs. You may be falling into the savings trap if...

- you feel guilt or pain every time you spend your money, even though you can easily afford it.
- you are not giving at least 10 percent of your money away.
- you have so much saved or invested that at your current lifestyle, you would have to live past 100 to spend it all!
- you constantly ridicule your children for spending instead of saving.
- your focus is on someday rather than today, with your primary focus being on retirement.
- your least favorite Bible passage is the story of the rich fool.
- you will spend one hour of your time to save two dollars on a purchase.
- you think anyone who spends money on a vacation is foolish.
- you consistently tip less than 15 percent when you eat out.

- you are always suspicious that people are out to get your money.
- all your investments are cautious; you believe that certificates of deposits are risky.
- your thoughts are dominated by money matters.
- you're overinsured with disability insurance, accidental death insurance, a cancer policy, and so much life insurance that your premature death would make your survivors much richer than they ever would have been otherwise.

WHY PEOPLE HOARD MONEY

The irony of the savings trap is that it usually snares those we assume are the least likely to have money problems. The wealthier a person is, the more likely he is to fall into this trap. He has plenty, but he keeps on saving, watching his investments, pinching every penny, and stockpiling money. Why? Here are the most common reasons I hear from people who hoard their money.

Reason 1: I Want to Feel Secure

People who hoard tend to be afraid of the future, thinking the economy could collapse, their health could fail, their retirement fund might be insufficient. They assume if they could save enough money, their worries would go away. "I just want enough so I won't have to worry," they say.

But money doesn't bring security or freedom from worry. Generally, the more money a person has, the more anxiety he feels. W. H. Vanderbilt said of his wealth, "The care of $200 million is too great for any brain or back to bear. It is enough to kill anyone. There is no pleasure in it."

Dr. Aaron Beck and his associates did a ten-year study of patients hospitalized with suicidal intentions, the results of which he then published in *The American Journal of Psychiatry*. One of the fifteen major risk factors contributing to a suicidal frame of mind was listed simply as "financial resources." Dr. Beck's terse commentary was, "Risk increases with resources."

Andrew Carnegie said, "Millionaires rarely smile."

Solomon, one of the wealthiest men of all time, said, "The sleep of a laborer is sweet, whether he eats little or much, but the abundance of a rich man permits him no sleep" (Ecclesiastes 5:12).

Reason 2: I Want to Feel Important

Many people stockpile their wealth because they think it will give them recognition and respect in society, thus enhancing their feelings of self-worth.

I took a short-term mission trip to Kenya, Africa, several years ago and visited the Masai, a very primitive tribe. Since the Masai determine worth by the size of their herds, many of them will hoard their cattle. They will sometimes own herds of cattle worth hundreds of thousands of dollars, but they choose to live in mud huts, wear garments that are old and smelly, and eat barely enough food to keep themselves alive. Their desire to feel important is stronger than their desire to live more comfortably.

In our society, a person's value is often tied to his net worth. If a person is "worth over a million dollars," then he is valuable. Money is a way of keeping score. If someone has more than we do, we feel intimidated. If we have more than others, we feel important.

Proverbs 11:26 says, "People curse the man who hoards grain." The person who hoards thinks he is impressing people but is more likely offending them instead.

John Rebutts, the recent chairman of AT&T, had one million employees. Several presidents of the United States frequently called him for advice. He had wealth, fame, and influence. But when he became severely ill and had to spend several days in the hospital, no one visited him, no one phoned, no one sent him cards. He said, "The only one there for me was the one person I had largely ignored for thirty years—my wife." Money will never provide what is truly important.

Rudyard Kipling once told a graduating class, "Someday you will meet a man who has no love for money, and then you'll realize how poor you really are."

Reason 3: I Was Raised to Be Frugal

Some of us grew up with parents who lived through the Depression. They drilled into us the value of a dollar and the need to squeeze every penny. "A penny saved is a penny earned," they would say. Or, "A fool and his money are soon parted." Your parents may have even scolded you for spending money frivolously or losing it.

For the most part, frugality is a positive trait, but there is a difference between being frugal and hoarding money. The frugal person is concerned that nothing be wasted. Jesus commanded his disciples to round up the leftover loaves and fishes after he fed the five thousand, saying, "Let nothing be wasted" (John 6:12). Frugality, however, can be taken to extremes. We tease one of my daughters-in-law because she will save her paper napkin and reuse it at the next meal. That's frugal, but it's not as bad as the man who reuses his dental floss!

Forbes magazine, in a story about famous tightwads, tried to define the difference between being frugal and being cheap. They identified some wealthy Americans who were notoriously cheap. J. Paul Getty made visitors use a pay phone in his home. Averell Harriman would look for parking meters with time left on them. Lee Iacocca used to buy himself a lavish Christmas gift and then charge his underlings for its cost. Ty Cobb collected used soap bits from the locker room shower stalls and sent them to the share-croppers on his farms. Cary Grant, called "El Squeako" in Hollywood, would keep count of the fire logs in his garage. Franklin D. Roosevelt would bum dollars from his valet for the church collection.[2]

If we stockpile things or money to an extreme, or for selfish reasons, we are refusing to use our God-given resources for the good of others or even for our own enjoyment. In the process we stifle the Lord and miss out on some of the greatest blessings of life.

A friend told me that his parents, who were both in their eighties, had plenty of money in savings, but his mother had to hide her Social Security check when it came to keep her husband from taking it to the bank and saving it. It was his habit to save all he could, although he never really stopped to ask why.

Maybe your family has always been frugal, and you don't know how to behave any differently. But the habit may be staying with you after the practicality has gone.

Reason 4: I Want to Be Generous Later

Some people want to make a lot of money so they can give a lot away later in life. They think, "I'm going to be a generous benefactor. I'll save as much as I can now, then start a charity for handicapped children." That's noble and would be a wonderful thing to do if God continues to bless them. But that's not usually the way it happens. Unless generosity is practiced consistently along the way, it is seldom practiced later in life because the habits are formed. God wants us to be obedient and generous now, not just in the future. Then, if God continues to bless us, we can begin thinking of more creative ways to give it away.

Randy Alcorn has said, "I'm called to live fully in each day, not in the future. Therefore, God evaluates the faithfulness of my management based on what I do with what I have now, not what I might do someday if I had more."

Reason 5: I Want My Children to Have an Inheritance

The hoarder might truly be unselfish and think, "I want my children and grandchildren to have enough so they can be secure." It sounds great, even biblical.

Once after I preached a sermon against hoarding, my sons reminded me of Proverbs 13:22, which says, "A good man leaves an inheritance for his children's children." That can be good if done wisely. But be careful that you don't endanger your children or grandchildren by hoarding your money, then leaving them too much to handle after you're gone.

THE PROBLEM WITH HOARDING

James gives us a vivid depiction of what will happen to those who are rich and who hoard their riches: "Now listen, you rich people, weep and wail because of the misery that is coming upon you. Your wealth has rotted, and moths have eaten your clothes. Your gold and silver are corroded. Their corrosion will testify against you and eat your flesh like fire. You have hoarded wealth in the last days. Look! The wages you failed to pay the workmen who mowed your fields are crying out against you. The cries of the harvesters have reached the ears of the Lord Almighty" (James 5:1–4).

Is that what we're saving for? It is so foolish to put our trust in things and hoard our money, never allowing God to use us to be generous to those in need, to spread the gospel, or even to bring joy to those around us.

I like what one poor man had put on his tombstone: "Being of sound mind, I spent it all." What are you saving it for? Who wants to be a hoarder? A friend of mine says he is always giving money away or spending it because he knows God has commanded him not to store up treasures on this earth. He's afraid Jesus will come back and catch him with some left over!

The real problem with hoarding is a failure to trust God. That's what was wrong with the rich farmer in Jesus' parable. He never mentioned God. He spoke of "*my* crops...*my* barns...all *my* grain." He even commented, "I will say to *myself.*" (Luke 12:16–19). He didn't say, "God has given me a great harvest," or "God will take care of me in the future." He didn't say, "I will express my thanks to God by giving some away." He was determined to provide completely for himself. Money had become his god.

When we hoard our money, we are attempting to control our own future. Jesus said, "Don't worry about tomorrow. God clothes the grass of the field and provides for the birds of the air. He will take care of you."

Said the robin to the sparrow,
"I would really like to know
Why those anxious human beings
Rush about and worry so."

Said the sparrow to the robin,
"I think that it must be
They have no Heavenly Father
Such as cares for you and me."[3]

OVERCOMING THE SAVINGS TRAP

If you are inclined to be a hoarder, recognize the danger and ask the Lord to help you change your attitude toward possessions. Don't just say, "That's the way I am." Pray to the Lord and ask for an attitude adjustment. Decide to change your thinking and begin to do things God's way. Here are three essential steps to overcoming the savings trap.

Step 1: Put Your Trust in God

Jesus said, "Therefore I tell you, do not worry about your life, what you will eat; or about your body, what you will wear.... Consider how the lilies grow. They do not labor or spin. Yet I tell you, not even Solomon in all his splendor was dressed like one of these. If that is how God clothes the grass of the field, which is here today, and tomorrow is thrown into the fire, how much more will he clothe you, O you of little faith!" (Luke 12:22, 27–28).

But the hoarder is always asking "what if...?" "What if there is inflation? What if I get sick? What if I lose my job?" Jesus commanded us to quit worrying and put our trust in God. The world may think that's ridiculous, but God's Word never fails. Quit trying to save up to prepare for any potential disaster or emergency that might come your way, and begin trusting God to meet your needs.

Step 2: Number Your Days

We usually view life in a rearview mirror. We count the number of years from our birth, adding up as we go along in life. Many people never consider how many years they have left on this earth, and thus don't plan accordingly. The average life span of an American is just under eighty years. If you are forty years old and in good health, you could likely live another forty years. The Bible says we should be aware that no man knows the hour of Christ's return, and God has not promised all of us the same number of years on this earth. But in planning for the future, we would be wise to consider the best- and worst-case scenarios. We could die tomorrow, or we could live to be a hundred.

The psalmist said, "Teach us to number our days aright, that we may gain a heart of wisdom" (Psalm 90:12). Consider the most years you can realistically expect to live, and use that number to plan the rest of your life. If you like, plan to live to a hundred. Sit down with a pencil and paper and number your days. If you live to be a hundred years old, how many years do you have left? How long can you expect to be productive in your current occupation or a similar job? If you are the CEO of a major corporation and you must travel a lot and bear much stress, you won't be able to keep up the same pace for the rest of your life. If you and a few partners have a smaller business that is low maintenance, you might be able to work longer. How much do you realistically need for retirement? How much do you have available to you—through savings, stocks, assets, and cash-value life insurance policies? How much do you really need to leave to your children or grandchildren?

After you have determined these things, create a savings plan. You may need some counsel from a financial expert, but only accept the counsel he or she gives that fits your goals. Don't let your financial adviser convince you there may be a worldwide catastrophe and you need to save more than you know you need.

Do you believe you can keep working for thirty more years? Determine a scale of savings, no more than you really need to reach your goals for your family and your retirement. Give away everything you earn beyond your needs. Remember that it is God's money, and he has made you responsible for it for reasons other than your own benefit. Don't just hoard it and use the excuse that you earned it and can do with it whatever you please. God has bigger plans for that money, and you should feel honored that he has chosen you as the channel of distribution.

Step 3: Give Away the Surplus

Get with an attorney and write out a will. Without a will, the state determines what will happen to your money and, more importantly, who will be the guardian of your children if they are still in your care. In your will, make provisions for the guardianship of your children, then take care of them financially. Leave a specified amount to your children and grandchildren, enough to help them and not be a burden to them. Then determine that you will give the rest away to a charitable organization. I prefer the church, of course!

Depending on your level of income, you may be wise to consider some type of charitable remainder trust. Such a trust still assures that your heirs will have a nice inheritance, whatever you specify, but the owner of the trust is the charity to which you want to leave the remainder. At your death, the charity receives a generous endowment and is bound by law to pay whatever you have specified to your heirs on an annual basis. The benefit of such a trust is that not only do your heirs and your charity gain from your generosity, but you are also sheltered from an estate tax burden that can eat an enormous amount of money—up to 50 percent—out of what you have saved. In many cases, the heirs actually receive a greater inheritance than they would have otherwise. Talk with your tax adviser, financial counselor, or attorney about a charitable remainder trust.

But I feel there's an even better way to give away your surplus—give it away while you are still alive. It takes faith to say, "I trust God to take care of me, and I won't stockpile for the future anymore," but it is a better way to give. Not only are you able to enjoy the thrill of giving, but you also maintain a level of influence over the institution to which you are giving. I know of people who at their death left millions for a college that they thought upheld basic Christian beliefs, but the school became liberal and began teaching the opposite. If the benefactor knew what they were teaching, he would roll over in his grave. Someone has said, "Do your giving while you're living, then you're knowing where it's going!"

In 1901 Andrew Carnegie sold his steel company to J. P. Morgan for two hundred million dollars. On that day Carnegie became the richest man in the world. But he spent the rest of his life trying to give away his entire fortune, most of it for educational purposes. He would say, "The man who dies rich dies disgraced."

Even billionaire Ted Turner has begun to admit it is more blessed to give than to receive. In a *New York Times* story entitled "Sharing the Wealth," Turner expressed his disdain for the billionaires of the world who refuse to give any money away. He said that instead of the *Forbes* list of the four hundred wealthiest Americans, someone should print a list of the most generous Americans. Turner got angry after reading a *New York Times* story revealing that the megarich give away a smaller percentage annually than the less fortunate do. "I was outraged," he said. "Haven't they ever seen Dickens's *A Christmas Carol?* Scrooge felt a lot happier when he saved Tiny Tim and bought the turkey for the poor family, right?"

Turner said he had tried to persuade Bill Gates and Warren Buffett, two of the richest men in the country, to be more generous. "What difference does it make if you're worth $12 billion or $11 billion?" he asked the two billionaires. "With a billion dollars you can build a whole university."[4]

Turner's motives for giving might not be perfect, but he has discovered how silly it is to hoard money.

Jesus commanded, "Do not store up for yourselves treasures on earth, where moth and rust destroy, and where thieves break in and steal. But store up for yourselves treasures in heaven, where moth and rust do not destroy, and where thieves do not break in and steal. For where your treasure is, there your heart will be also" (Matthew 6:19–21).

Decide you are going to store treasures in heaven rather than foolishly hoard them here on earth.

CHAPTER TEN

THE WISEST INVESTMENTS

A good man leaves an inheritance for his children's children, but a sinner's wealth is stored up for the righteous.

PROVERBS 13:22

He who provides for this life but takes no care for eternity is wise for a moment but a fool forever.

JOHN TILLOTSON, ARCHBISHOP OF CANTERBURY

Imagine you were living in the South during the Civil War and had accumulated a large amount of Confederate currency. Suppose you had known for a fact that the North was going to win soon and your money would be useless. What would you have done with your Confederate money? If you were smart, you would have cashed in your Confederate currency for US currency, the only money that would have value once the war was over. You would have kept only enough Confederate money to meet your basic needs until the war was over.

The Christian has insider information on a coming worldwide change in our social and economic situation. The currency of this world will be worthless when we die or Christ returns—both of which are imminent. That knowledge should radically affect our investment strategy. For us to accumulate vast earthly treasures in the face of the inevitable future is equivalent to stockpiling Confederate money despite our awareness of its eventual worthlessness. To do so is to betray our belief in the Scriptures.

There are hundreds of financial advisers making thousands of dollars by counseling us as to which investments are the wisest. But Jesus commanded us not to go to so much effort "storing up treasures" on this earth that is temporal. Instead, we should "store up treasures in heaven" (Matthew 6:20).

I heard a story about a wealthy man who begged God for the privilege of taking his money with him when he died. He was so persistent that the Lord finally gave in and said, "All right, you can bring one sack with you when you come." The man liquidated all his assets and transferred them into gold bars.

When he died, he stood before Saint Peter with his sack of gold. Peter said, "I'm sorry, but you can't bring anything with you."

The man said, "I have special permission from the Lord himself to bring this one sack."

Peter looked inside the sack, then telephoned the Lord. He said, "There's a guy out here who insists you gave him permission to bring one sack with him. But for the life of me, I can't figure out why he would want to bring pavement!"

Heaven is described as a land where the streets are paved with gold. It will be a place of such great riches that whatever we have stockpiled on this earth will seem like pavement by comparison. One of the compelling reasons to give our money away should be to "store up treasures in heaven." As a wise old preacher said, "You can't take it with you, but you can send it on ahead!"

Here are three investments we can make in heavenly treasures.

INVESTMENT 1: THE NEEDY

The Bible makes special provisions for the poor. The Old Testament instructed wealthy farmers to be sensitive to the poor at harvest time. They were not to go back over their fields and harvest what was missed the first time. Instead, the reapers were to leave some grain standing so the poor could gather the leftovers.

Deuteronomy says, "If there is a poor man among your brothers in any of the towns of the land that the LORD your God is giving you, do not be hardhearted or tightfisted toward your poor brother. Rather be openhanded and freely lend him whatever he needs" (15:7–8).

Proverbs goes so far as to say, "He who is kind to the poor

lends to the LORD, and he will reward him for what he has done" (19:17).

Jesus also taught that the rich have a responsibility to be generous to the poor:

> "Give to the one who asks you, and do not turn away from the one who wants to borrow from you." (Matthew 5:42)

> "Then the King will say to those on his right, 'Come, you who are blessed by my Father; take your inheritance, the kingdom prepared for you since the creation of the world. For I was hungry and you gave me something to eat, I was thirsty and you gave me something to drink, I was a stranger and you invited me in, I needed clothes and you clothed me, I was sick and you looked after me, I was in prison and you came to visit me.'
>
> "Then the righteous will answer him, 'Lord, when did we see you hungry and feed you, or thirsty and give you something to drink? When did we see you a stranger and invite you in, or needing clothes and clothe you? When did we see you sick or in prison and go to visit you?'
>
> "The King will reply, 'I tell you the truth, whatever you did for one of the least of these brothers of mine, you did for me.'" (Matthew 25:34–40)

The Jerusalem church had its own welfare system to provide for the widows and orphans: "There were no needy persons among them. For from time to time those who owned lands or houses sold them, brought the money from the sales and put it at the apostles' feet, and it was distributed to anyone as he had need" (Acts 4:34–35).

The New Testament writers also teach us to care for the needy: "If anyone has material possessions and sees his brother in need but has no pity on him, how can the love of God be in him?" (1 John 3:17).

The Bible couldn't make it any clearer. Those who have been given resources are to share with those in need. It is a sin against God and against our fellowman to hoard our riches and ignore the needs of those around us. On the other hand, God promises to honor our sensitivity, compassion, and generosity toward the needy.

But there are so many needy people. How do we know whom to support? Since we can't help everyone in need, we don't want to give money to someone who is not deserving.

First John 4:1 says, "Dear friends, do not believe every spirit, but test the spirits to see whether they are from God, because many false prophets have gone out into the world." Just because someone asks for a donation doesn't mean we should give. We could be supporting a bad habit or an immoral cause if we're not discerning. Before we give, we should ask these questions:

Is this person or organization in need? The Bible instructs us to take care of others' needs, not to give them everything they want. People have asked our church to help with college tuition, credit card payments, and transportation costs. We've had people call our church to ask for one of our Thanksgiving baskets and then say, "Do you have any meat in your baskets? If not, I might call someplace else." It's hard to get excited about giving to a person who may not really be in need. Our church tries to provide physical necessities—food, clothing, and shelter—to those who are truly in need, then provide financial counseling and support for the rest.

Is this person willing to work? The New Testament gives the following welfare guideline: "If a man will not work, he shall not eat" (2 Thessalonians 3:10). An unemployed man who asks our church for financial assistance but refuses to show up for a job interview will be denied further assistance. We are not to help those who refuse to help themselves. If you see someone on the side of the road with a sign "Will work for food," offer him the opportunity to work. If he is telling you the truth, he will be willing to work, and you will have given him a sense of dignity by not just giving him a handout.

Will the money be used to meet the intended need? If you're wondering whether the money might be used to buy drugs or alcohol instead of groceries, go to the extra trouble of buying food to give, so there's no doubt. If you're wondering whether the organization asking for money is giving to the needy or is pocketing most of the income, take the time to check it out before you give.

Is this cause worthy of my support? You don't want to give generously only to have your funds support an anti-Christian cause or organization. One of our good neighbors came by, soliciting for a well-known organization. I remembered it from years ago as one that fought polio, which has been virtually conquered, praise the Lord. Now they say that the funds are used to eliminate crippling diseases. I wrote out a ten-dollar check. Two days later someone showed me a book by George Grant entitled *Grand Illusions,* in which he documents that a significant portion of the money donated to that organization goes into the coffers of Planned Parenthood, a group that funds abortion. The money I thought I had given to eliminate crippling diseases is used to eliminate births. Consequently, I won't give to that organization anymore.

The best way to give to the needy is to find an individual or family you know is in need and do something for them on a regular basis. Through our crisis pregnancy center, my son and his wife found a young single mother on welfare who needed help. They bought her some basic items that she needed, gave clothes for her children, and tried to develop a relationship with her family. They have given her Christmas gifts for the past several years and have attempted to maintain the relationship. As a result, she and her family have visited our church. That type of benevolence takes more effort, but it has much better results. There is more accountability, and it is more meaningful for both the giver and the receiver.

INVESTMENT 2: OUR CHILDREN

Most parents plan to leave their children all their earthly goods when they die. That's understandable, but it can be unwise. We know it's not wrong to attempt to care for those we love after we're gone, since Jesus, when he was dying, made provisions for the apostle John to take care of his mother. But we usually overdo it with our inheritance.

A couple accumulates a few earthly goods in this life, and then at age eighty or eighty-five both die, and an executor divides up the estate among the two or three descendants. That is often a tense time, occasionally producing hard feelings. Much of the inheritance will be eaten up in estate taxes and lawyers' fees. Children seldom appreciate the money as much as the parents hoped they would.

The time to give your money to your children is when they are younger. Here are several reasons.

The money is truly a benefit to them. If you leave your money to your children when you're eighty or ninety, your kids will be fifty years old or older. Their greater need is in their younger years, when you're reaching your peak earning period and they are just starting out. When they're first married or purchasing their first home or raising children—those are their times of need. One banker revealed that 96 percent of first-time home buyers need financial assistance from their parents in order to complete the transaction.

After preaching a sermon on this topic a few years ago, I got a letter from a young couple in our church. The wife's father had been touched by the message and had sent each of his three children two thousand dollars, explaining his motivation. The young couple thanked me for inspiring the father's generosity. "We call it the six-thousand-dollar sermon!" they said.

You can enjoy it with them. If I give while my children are younger, I can enjoy seeing them benefit from my generosity. I get to see their new home or the new toys for my grandkids. Conversely, if I refuse to be generous while I'm alive, I might wonder if the kids would be happier if I checked out early.

They might be like the young boy who kept asking his grandfather to make the sound of a frog. "Why do you want me to sound like a frog?" the grandfather finally asked.

"Because I heard Mom say that when you croak, we'll all be rich!" he responded.

Once when Jesus was dining with his disciples, their friend Mary took a very expensive jar of perfume—worth one year's wages—and broke it, pouring the contents on Jesus' feet to express her love for him. The disciples protested that it was wasteful, that she could have sold the perfume and given the money to the poor.

But Jesus said, "Leave her alone. It was intended that she should save this perfume for the day of my burial. You will always have the poor among you, but you will not always have me" (John 12:7–8).

There are times when it is appropriate to "break a jar" and give generously to those around you to express your love for them.

It is a tax advantage. I can give ten thousand dollars a year to each of my children without it being an additional tax burden. (Trust me, I have never violated that gift level!)

However, if a person waits until he dies, his estate is going to be taxed heavily and immediately, at a minimum rate of 18 percent for everything above six hundred thousand dollars, up to a maximum level of 55 percent for everything above three million. Six hundred thousand dollars may seem like a large amount of money, but that includes all of one's assets—life insurance, house, vehicles, jewelry, stocks, pension plans. All of them have an appraised value and will be taxed at the appraised rate immediately.

You are wise either to shift your assets into a charitable trust so your heirs pay no taxes or to begin giving away your assets now. (Or better still, do both.)

You can keep them accountable. If you hoard your money while you're living and then leave a large inheritance to your kids, you can't control how they will spend it. We shouldn't put qualifiers on our gifts, but neither should we continue supporting immoral behavior. If a son or daughter begins using our money for evil instead of good, we have the right—and often the duty—to stop giving.

You can teach them to be good stewards. When you give your children money, you have the opportunity to teach them how to use it wisely. Moses told the Israelites, "Fix these words of mine in your hearts and minds.... Teach them to your children" (Deuteronomy 11:18–19). It is our God-given responsibility to teach our children God's principles. We can do so by giving them progressive amounts of money while they are still at home and helping them budget their funds.

Mike Breaux, the preacher at the Southland Christian Church in Lexington, Kentucky, entrusts his children with a designated amount of money from each paycheck. The money is to go toward lunches at school, entertainment, savings, extra clothes, and church. He gives twenty dollars to the six-year-old, forty to the nine-year-old, and seventy to the twelve-year-old. When that money is gone, they are not to ask for more but are to wait until the next paycheck. They are also given five envelopes, with the following designations: (1) Jesus (they are encouraged to give 10 percent to the church), (2) savings, (3) gifts for others, such as birthdays and Christmas, (4) clothing, and (5) spending, to include lunches, entertainment, etc.

Mike said, "At the end of the first month, we were returning from a youth outing and stopped at McDonald's. My nine-year-old son had no money for lunch because he had blown it at the arcade earlier that day. When he asked me for money, it was hard to say, 'No, I'm not giving you any more. You'll have to wait until you get home and fix yourself a sandwich.' That was not a 'Happy Meal!' I felt terrible. But I stood my ground, remembering the management principle, 'If failed performance is rewarded, failed performance will be repeated.'" Breaux's son quickly learned to manage his money, and the next month he was wiser.

Such methods can be followed too rigidly and provoke children to anger, but a wise parent will develop a system to teach his children how to be faithful stewards. They will thank you later, and you will have given them something more important than money, thus storing up more treasures in heaven.

THE WISEST INVESTMENT: THE LOCAL CHURCH

The best investment you can make is to give your money to the kingdom of God through your local church. But how much should we give to the local church?

The Old Testament demanded that the Jews give 10 percent of their profits back to God: "A tithe of everything from the land, whether grain from the soil or fruit from the trees, belongs to the LORD; it is holy to the LORD" (Leviticus 27:30). The word *tithe* means "10 percent." The tithe was not considered a gift to God; it belonged to God, and the Jews were stealing from God not to give it to him.

> "Will a man rob God? Yet you rob me.
> "But you ask, 'How do we rob you?'
> "In tithes and offerings. You are under a curse—the whole nation of you—because you are robbing me. Bring the whole tithe into the storehouse, that there may be food in my house. Test me in this," says the LORD

Almighty, "and see if I will not throw open the floodgates of heaven and pour out so much blessing that you will not have room enough for it." (Malachi 3:8–10)

Notice that the tithe was not just to be given away but was specifically to be brought into the storehouse (the temple), where it would be distributed by the priest.

Under the new covenant through Christ, we are no longer bound by the Old Testament law. As Scripture reveals, "For sin shall not be your master, because you are not under law, but under grace" (Romans 6:14) and "God made you alive with Christ. He forgave us all our sins, having canceled the written code, with its regulations, that was against us and that stood opposed to us; he took it away, nailing it to the cross" (Colossians 2:13–15).

In the New Testament church, the standard for giving is grace, not the law. The tithe command is not repeated anywhere in the New Testament. Instead, we are given the following command about stewardship. "Remember this: Whoever sows sparingly will also reap sparingly, and whoever sows generously will also reap generously. Each man should give what he has decided in his heart to give, not reluctantly or under compulsion, for God loves a cheerful giver. And God is able to make all grace abound to you, so that in all things at all times, having all that you need, you will abound in every good work" (2 Corinthians 9:6–8).

That scripture contains three principles for giving to our local church.

PRINCIPLE 1: GIVE GENEROUSLY

Some people decide how much to give to the church by comparing it to entertainment. A ball game costs twelve dollars, a movie costs seven dollars, a ticket to an amusement park costs twenty dollars. Using that standard, if I'm generous, I'll give twenty dollars a week to the church. But even though we are no longer bound by the Old Testament law, the measuring stick of "generous" is still the Old Testament tithe.

Often when I go out to eat in a restaurant in our town, the waitress will say, "Hello, Bob." Immediately I know two things: She knows who I am, and I had better leave a generous tip.

If you are served well by the waiter or waitress at the restaurant—he pays extra attention to your table and is especially courteous—what would you consider to be a generous tip? That depends on two things: the amount of the bill and the standard of generosity. Three dollars would be considered a generous tip if the bill came to ten dollars. But three dollars would be miserly if the bill came to forty dollars, because the acceptable standard for tipping is 15 percent. A generous tip for a meal would be more than 15 percent of the bill.

God is not serving us; we are serving him. In the Old Testament there was a minimum standard we were to return to him—10 percent. Then in the New Testament, he gives us Jesus Christ, the Holy Spirit, the church, freedom from the law, and the promise of eternal life. And God says, in essence, "You give as generously as you have been blessed." If the tithe was the minimum standard in the Old Testament, what is considered to be generous in the New Testament? I would consider it to be more than 10 percent.

Most of us have been blessed extravagantly—with good health, loved ones, good jobs, and nice houses. We have the spiritual blessings of salvation, the church, the Holy Spirit, forgiveness of sins, and the promise of eternal life. After all God has given to us, can we be satisfied giving 3 or 4 percent of our income when God's standard of generosity begins at 10 percent?

That may seem radical to many Christians, but I've learned that there are two kinds of givers: those who give by *reason*, and those who give by *revelation*. If you give by reason, you calculate how much you will give by how much you can afford to give. If you give by revelation, you say, "How much does God expect me to give?" and then you obey, trusting him to provide the rest.

I heard about a bumper sticker that said, "Tithe if you love Jesus. Anybody can honk!" To tithe your income may be a huge step for you, but if you believe in the Lord's promise, you will trust him to provide.

The world measures worth by how much you make. If you're a Christian, why not measure your financial worth by how much you're able to give away?

Statistics concur with Christ's statement that it's hard for a rich man to enter heaven. The more money people make, the smaller the percentage of their income they give to charities. The following statistics appeared in the National Association of Church Business newsletter:

- Those making less than ten thousand dollars a year give more than 5 percent to charity.
- Those making fifty thousand to one hundred thousand dollars a year give 3.2 percent to charity.
- Those making more than a hundred thousand dollars give 2.9 percent to charity.

That's pitiful! But it demonstrates the danger of riches. The more we make, the more we tend to trust in riches, and the harder it may be for us to give our money away.

An even more accurate gauge of our generosity is the *level of sacrifice*. Jesus watched people tossing money into the treasury and saw the Pharisees giving what seemed like a lot of money. But he knew they were giving out of their great wealth. A woman who had only two mites dropped them both in the offering, and Jesus said, "She has given the most, because she gave all that she had" (see Luke 21:4). Jesus measured her generosity by how much she kept for herself. By that standard, I have a long way to go before I am considered a generous giver.

PRINCIPLE 2: GIVE WILLFULLY

Bob Hope says there was a time when he and Jack Benny were in the car together and came to a toll booth. Hope was driving and asked Benny if he had a dollar for the toll. Benny reluctantly handed him a twenty-dollar bill, saying, "I don't have any ones." Hope handed the twenty-dollar bill to the toll keeper and said, "Keep the change!"

Jack Benny was generous, but he wasn't giving willfully. You could say, "Thirty-five percent of my income is deducted for taxes, and on what I'm making, I'm probably supporting two or three welfare recipients. Besides that, our company deducts a portion each year to give to the United Way. Then I purchase my gas at a station that gives a percentage to the Crusade for Children." But that isn't generous giving when you don't give of your own free will.

I was once sitting on the platform at a large gathering, preparing to speak, when an audacious preacher appealed for the offering and said, "Make sure to bring that offering plate up here to the platform. These guys need to be giving, too!"

Suddenly I was put on the spot. I wasn't going to fail to give in front of ten thousand people. I looked in my wallet, and the smallest bill I had was a twenty. That was a lot of money to me, but I dropped it in—not because I was generous, but because my pride was more important than the twenty dollars!

Jesus warned, "Be careful not to do your 'acts of righteousness' before men, to be seen by them. If you do, you will have no reward from your Father in heaven. So when you give to the needy, do not announce it with trumpets, as the hypocrites do in the synagogues and on the streets, to be honored by men. I tell you the truth, they have received their reward in full. But when you give to the needy, do not let your left hand know what your right hand is doing, so that your giving may be in secret. Then your Father, who sees what is done in secret, will reward you" (Matthew 6:1–4).

God knows your heart. Don't give out of reluctance or compulsion. Give willfully.

PRINCIPLE 3: GIVE CHEERFULLY

Imagine what would happen if I took my wife a gift on our anniversary, tossed it in her lap, and said, "Here. The kids said I better buy you something or you would pout for weeks. It cost too much, but I hope you're satisfied."

Would she respond by saying, "Oh, thank you! You're such a wonderful husband. How thoughtful of you"? If she did, there would be something wrong with her mind! No one wants to receive a gift given grudgingly or out of compulsion. Giving ought to be fun. The word Paul uses for *cheerful* in the phrase "God loves a cheerful giver" is the Greek word from which we get the word *hilarious*. God loves a gift that blesses both the giver and the receiver because it is done out of generosity and love.

I heard about a fund-raising dinner where a couple testified they were giving a thousand dollars to the organization in the name of their son who was killed in Vietnam.

A middle-aged mother sitting in the audience leaned toward her husband and said, "Let's give a thousand dollars in memory of our son."

"Why?" he asked. "Our son wasn't killed in Vietnam!"

"That's just it," she smiled. "Let's give out of gratitude that he is alive and healthy. We have so much to be thankful for."

Several years ago, just before our first relocation project, we felt God was calling us to find land and build a new church building. We found twenty-two acres less than a half-mile from our original site, a perfect location for us to build. But it was going to cost more than two hundred thousand dollars for the land and ten million for the facility. The elders planned to ask the congregation for a special, one-million-dollar offering so the project could continue.

After we debated for a while in a board meeting over how to raise the money needed immediately to purchase the land, one of our elders said, "I think we can raise the money for the land among ourselves. It would be a great example to the church of sacrificial giving if we could say that the families of the elders and deacons raised the money for the property. I've done some calculating, and it comes to three thousand dollars per family among the board. Are there any questions?"

There were a few timid questions, then we voted it through. We decided to give the money in cash, to be received at the next month's meeting. We walked out the door asking, "What did we just do?" We didn't have a lot of rich people on the board. We had a couple of schoolteachers and some people living off limited, retirement income. Some were really concerned they couldn't hold up their end of the bargain.

But throughout the month, we began hearing stories of sacrifice. One man was selling his house and moving to a smaller one. Another was selling his second car. Some were canceling vacations, and others were taking out second mortgages. Three families borrowed ten thousand dollars to give beyond what was asked of them.

The next month there was a mood of anticipation as everyone gathered for the board meeting. One of our elders came wearing sunglasses, carrying a cane, and holding a tin cup! After the pledges were counted, it was announced that we had given not two hundred thousand dollars, but two hundred and fifty thousand dollars! Everyone rejoiced. We wept and sang and prayed that night. If anyone had walked into the room, he would have thought we had all just inherited several thousand dollars. But we had given it away.

On the way out the door, one man hollered, "I'll be shining shoes outside."

"What shoes?" another responded.

We had sacrificed deeply, but we had discovered the joy of sacrificial giving.

God wants our giving to flow from joyful, generous hearts, out of gratitude for what he has done for us.

COMMON QUESTIONS ABOUT TITHING

Whenever I suggest that people should tithe their income, I invariably am asked these questions:

Should I tithe the gross or net of my income? Should a person use his gross income before taxes or his take-home pay after taxes in calculating the percentage? My answer? "It depends on whether you want a gross or net reward!" I feel the tithe should be taken from our income before taxes and benefits. We benefit from the taxes we pay—by the roads we use, police protection, schools, garbage collection, etc. Jesus said, "Give to Caesar what is Caesar's and to God what is God's" (Matthew 22:21). The principle is that we should give the firstfruits.

Paul Harvey told about a woman who called the consumer hotline in her town to ask what she should do with the turkey she had found in her deep freeze. She said it had been there for twenty-three years! The hotline operator told her that if she had kept it frozen below zero degrees, the meat would not be unhealthy but that it wouldn't be good to eat because all the flavor would most likely be gone.

"That's what I thought," said the woman. "I'll just give it to the church."

Proverbs 3:9 says, "Honor the Lord with your wealth, with the *firstfruits* of all your crops."

Should all the tithe go to my local church? I feel that it should. If I choose to support individual causes or missions outside the church, it should be with a portion of my income beyond my tithe. The Bible refers to some gifts as "offerings" and separates them from the "tithe." The Jews were to bring the tithe into the storehouse, or the temple (Malachi 3:10). The Jerusalem Christians brought their gifts and laid them at the apostles' feet

(Acts 4:35). They also sent a gift intended for the church at Antioch to the *elders* of that church for distribution (Acts 11:30). When I give to the church, I am submitting to the oversight and wisdom of the church leadership. I am admitting that I am not as wise and discerning as the body of leadership God has designated in my church to determine what cause is the best to support.

Should I tithe if I can't pay my bills? If you can't afford the necessities of food, clothing, and shelter, I would say no. But make it your goal to tithe as soon as possible. Not being able to pay your bills should be only a short-term excuse for the new Christian or for someone who has just come to understand his need to give at this level. Get out of debt as soon as possible. In the meantime, immediately begin giving whatever you can to God every week— even if it seems minuscule—to show your obedience and your intention. I believe you will begin to see the blessings of God. Determine that within three years you will be a tither. Keep a journal of how God blesses you once you begin giving more, so that your faith will be reinforced. Then examine your budget and expenses each month to determine what you can do without so you can tithe. If someone claims he cannot tithe, but he has a cellular phone, a VCR, cable television, a boat, a vacation home, and a sizable savings account, he needs to reevaluate his priorities.

Should I tithe if my spouse is against it? No. Tithing should not cause a wedge in your marriage relationship. Talk it over with your spouse and come to an agreement. See if you can compromise. Give an agreed-upon gift each week for a year, and journal all of God's blessings during that time. When the year is up, look at the journal and see if you can increase your giving the next year.

Jesus said that where your treasure is, that is where your heart will be also (Matthew 6:21). A track coach once encouraged his pole vaulter, "Son, throw your heart over the bar and the rest of you will follow." Throw your heart into the kingdom of God, and your money will follow.

Max Lucado compares our efforts to build treasures on earth with a little child building a sandcastle. A little boy on the beach takes great pains in building a castle—spooning out the moat, packing the walls, getting Popsicle sticks for the bridges. Much to the delight of the boy, a castle is soon created.

A man in his office shuffles papers, delegates assignments, cradles his phone on his shoulder, and punches the keyboard with his fingers. Numbers are jotted down, contracts are signed, and much to his delight an empire is designed. All of his life he works, formulating plans, forecasting futures. Annuities will be his sentries; capital gains will be his bridges. An empire will be built.

Lucado writes,

Two builders of two castles. They have much in common. They shape granules into grandeurs. They see nothing and make something. They are diligent and determined. And for both the tide will rise and the end will come.

Yet, that is where the similarities cease. For the boy sees the end while the man ignores it. Watch the boy as the dusk approaches. Each wave slaps an inch closer to his creation....

But the boy doesn't panic. He is not surprised. All day the pounding waves have reminded him that the end is inevitable. He knows the secret of the surging. Soon they will come and take his castle into the deep.

The man, however, doesn't know the secret. He should. He, like the boy, lives surrounded by rhythmic reminders. Days come and go. Seasons ebb and flow. Every sunrise which becomes a sunset whispers the secret, "Time will take your castles."

So, one is prepared and one isn't....

As the waves near, the wise child jumps to his feet

and begins to clap. There is no sorrow. No fear. No regret. He knew this would happen.... And when the great breaker crashes into his castle and his masterpiece is sucked into the sea, he smiles. He smiles, picks up his tools, takes his father's hand, and goes home.

The grownup, however, is not so wise. As the wave of years collapses on his castle he is terrified. He hovers over the sandy monument to protect it. He blocks the waves from the walls he has made....

"It's my castle!" he defies.

The ocean need not respond. Both know to whom the sand belongs.

Lucado concludes:

Finally, the cliff of water mounts high above the man and his little empire. For just a moment he is shadowed by the wall of water...then it crashes. His tiny towers of triumph crumble and disperse and he is left on his knees...clutching muddy handfuls of yesterday.

If only he had known. If only he had listened. If only...[1]

Are you going to spend your time building sandy empires on this earth or treasures in heaven?

CHAPTER ELEVEN

TEST GOD IN THIS

Honor the LORD with your wealth,
with the firstfruits of all your crops;
then your barns will be filled to overflowing,
and your vats will brim over with new wine.

PROVERBS 3:9–10

The late Bob Benson used to tell about going to a Sunday school picnic. Everyone was supposed to bring their own lunch, but he was in a hurry, so he packed a bologna sandwich and a soft drink. When he arrived at the picnic, since he was alone, a family asked him to join them. They broke out a luscious meal—fried chicken, potato salad, baked beans, coleslaw, brownies for dessert—the works.

The family didn't want to embarrass Bob by saying, "Do you want some of our chicken?" Instead they said, "Bob, we always put all of our food together and share. If you would be willing to share your meal with us, we would like to share our meal with you." Benson jumped at the chance and was able to enjoy a wonderful picnic.[1]

The apostle Paul commanded us to be generous, then he promised: "And God is able to make all grace abound to you, so that in all things at all times, having all that you need, you will abound in every good work" (2 Corinthians 9:8).

God has all the riches of eternity at his disposal. We have a bologna sandwich, and we are foolish to hoard it. What we have is not much to brag about. God says, "If you are willing to share what you have, I will share with you my riches." And the Bible says he owns it all. Heaven and earth are his to disperse as he wishes. We are silly not to jump at the chance.

God makes at least four specific promises to those who are willing to give up their "bologna sandwiches."

SUCCESS IN OUR WORK

Deuteronomy says, "Give generously to him and do so without a grudging heart; then because of this the Lord your God will bless you in all your work and in everything you put your hand to" (15:10). When we are generous, God promises to bless our work.

About twelve years ago, a longtime member of our church, Ron Geary, asked to see me. Ron Geary had developed his own C.P.A. practice and had been very successful. Shortly after he turned thirty, he sold his practice and became the secretary of revenue in the cabinet of Kentucky's Governor John Y. Brown Jr. After four years of public service, Ron began to practice law. But he was really restless and unsatisfied.

Ron came to me and said, "Bob, I want my life to count for God. I'm not satisfied with what I'm doing right now. Will you pray with me that the Lord will make clear to me what he wants me to do?" We prayed together, then waited for the Lord's answer.

Six months later, Cincinnati Bible College was looking for a new president. The school was going through financially stressful times that were threatening to collapse the sixty-year-old institution. CBC is my alma mater, and since I was serving on the board of trustees at that time, I suggested that Ron be considered as a candidate. Within two months, he was appointed president of the college.

Taking that job required Ron to accept a drastic reduction in salary. He moved from a spacious suburban home to a small house near campus, almost in the inner city of Cincinnati. It was not an easy adjustment for him, but he did a tremendous job as president. Many credit him with saving the institution. Not only did he save it financially, by the grace of God, but he also helped to improve the academic standards and student enrollment while he was there.

About four years later, after the school was on sound financial ground again, the time came for CBC to return to a more traditional president with a background in ministry. Ron resigned his position.

At that juncture in his life, many of his resources had been depleted, and he was without a job. He sent out ninety-five résumés, but nothing happened. It was hard for him to understand what God had in mind for him next.

But just as he was about to buy a business in Iowa, hundreds of miles from home, he was offered a position as the CEO for a healthcare company headquartered in his hometown of Louisville.

Ron turned that company around too, so dramatically that within a few years, they went public with their stock. Once again Ron has been richly blessed financially and is a very charitable giver to a number of organizations.

Ron told me, "Every job I had, and especially the task I performed at Cincinnati Bible College, trained me to do the job I am now doing. God is faithful. God is good."

God rewards those who seek his will and who give of themselves and their finances. God's reward may not always be as dramatic as Ron has experienced. There are always other factors, and God may choose to bless us in other ways. But I believe God's promises are true. When we give generously of the money we make in honest work, God will bless that work. But there is a purpose. God blesses the work so we can continue to give. Paul said, "And God is able to make all grace abound to you, so that in all things at all times, having all that you need, you will abound in every good work" (2 Corinthians 9:8).

I heard about a man who gave his testimony at a missionary convention during the offering collection. He said, "I am living proof that God's promises come true. Many years ago, when I was just a boy at this missionary convention, the offering plate came around, and I only had one dollar. I gave all I had to the missionaries, and God has blessed me ever since. Today I am a millionaire."

He began to sit down when a woman in the middle of the audience stood up and said, "I dare you to do that again!"

God will bless your work so that you can do it again, continuing to give generously.

A GENEROUS RETURN ON OUR INVESTMENT

In an effort to illustrate the rewards we can expect from God for our generosity, Paul used the analogy of a farmer sowing seeds for his crop: "Remember this: Whoever sows sparingly will also reap sparingly, and whoever sows generously will also reap generously" (2 Corinthians 9:6).

One of our staff members, Brian Wright, grew up on a wheat farm in Oklahoma. I asked him how much wheat you can expect to reap per bushel of seed you plant. He said it depends on the condition of the land. In dry land, one bushel of wheat sown will yield about thirty bushels of wheat. If you sow one bushel in irrigated land, you can expect to reap over fifty bushels. That's a 5,000 percent return on our investment! And that's the illustration Paul used to describe the magnitude of God's blessings to us when we give generously.

Jesus promised, "Give, and it will be given to you. A good measure, pressed down, shaken together and running over, will be poured into your lap. For with the measure you use, it will be measured to you" (Luke 6:38). Have you ever opened a box of cereal or a bag of potato chips and been disappointed because the container is already half-empty? There is probably a disclaimer on the product that says the contents will not be filled to the top because you have to allow for "settling." Jesus said that when we give, God gives in return, "a good measure, pressed down, shaken together and running over."

The Bible commands us not to "test" the Lord (see Deuteronomy 6:16 and Matthew 4:7). But there is one exception. God almost dares us to test him in one area: the tithe. "'Bring the whole tithe into the storehouse, that there may be food in my house. Test me in this,' says the LORD Almighty, 'and see if I will not throw open the floodgates of heaven and pour out so much blessing that you will not have room enough for it'" (Malachi 3:10).

I have heard it said, "You cannot outgive God." I believe it. I've seen this principle demonstrated in my own life and in the lives of many others who tithe their income. Test God, and see if his principle is true.

The First Christian Church of Owasso, Oklahoma, made an offer to its people: "Try tithing for ninety days, and if you are not blessed, the church will refund your money." That's bold! But God will prove faithful. In fact, I'll give you the same guarantee. If you try tithing for ninety days and you are not blessed,...contact the First Christian Church of Owasso, Oklahoma, and they will refund your money!

However, God is not a genie, waiting around to give us everything we want just because we tithe. God's promised blessings have two qualifiers.

God's blessings take time. We don't sow a seed and then reap a bountiful harvest next week. It takes several long months for the seed to germinate and grow to maturity. Just because you begin tithing today doesn't mean you will automatically reap riches tomorrow. God will supply your need, but the bountiful harvest takes time to grow.

Not all God's blessings are material. God promises in 2 Corinthians 9:10 to enlarge the harvest of our *righteousness.* He does not promise to enlarge the harvest of our *bank accounts.* In the next sentence he promises that we will be made rich *in every way* (2 Corinthians 9:11).

The following quote from Benjamin Stein of the *American Spectator* provides a good definition of riches:

> How much money do you have to have to be considered rich in today's society? Some say about $1.3 million per family member. Others say about $5 million per family. Some individuals have told me you should have unearned income of about $500,000 per year to be considered rich.
>
> But I keep thinking of how many people I know with far more than that who do not seem happy. On the other hand, I know many people who have trouble paying their bills yet are really well off.
>
> If you can share any problem with your wife, you're rich. If you can face your parents and believe you have given back to them even a hint of what they gave you, you're rich. If you can take an afternoon off to go boating with your pal, you're rich. If you can honestly say you have nothing to hide, you are really, really rich.[2]

God often does bless us financially, but primarily he blesses us according to our spiritual needs. When we become generous, God rewards us with his spiritual riches:

- We are rich in promise. God promises us eternal life, more valuable than the riches of the whole world.
- We are rich in forgiveness. Our past is wiped clean through the sacrifice of Jesus Christ, and we are righteous in God's sight.
- We are rich in relationships. We have brothers and sisters in Christ who love us and care about us.
- We are rich in integrity. The Bible says a good name is worth more than rubies.

- We are rich in purpose. We have a reason to live: We want to go to heaven when we die and take as many people with us as we can.
- We are rich in generosity. We have learned the secret of money—that we don't earn to hoard but to share.
- We are rich in contentment. We have learned to be content whether we have little or much.

JOY BEYOND COMPARISON

The most surprising result of generous giving is joy. Jesus promised, "It is more blessed to give than to receive" (Acts 20:35). The word *blessed* can be translated *happy*. The Good News Bible translates Jesus as saying, "There is more happiness in giving than in receiving."

I've seen this promise come true many times in my own life. We are happier people when we give than when we receive. I remember one Christmas when my two sons were teenagers and had saved up to buy a generous Christmas present for my wife and me. They lugged in a large present the night before, making us promise not to enter the room where they were wrapping it. The next morning we opened up a new color television set! We were really grateful for such a nice gift, but we didn't have nearly as much fun receiving it as they did giving it. I was doubly glad that they had reached a point of maturity in their lives where they had discovered it is more blessed to give than to receive.

I discovered recently that a young couple in our church is giving away 50 percent of their income every year. They make about four hundred thousand dollars a year and determined they didn't need that much to live on. You might say, "Oh, sure, if I made that kind of money, I'd be that generous." But that is very rare. It's easy to think, *If I just saved a little more, I could retire early. I need a few hundred thousand more to cover the education expenses for my children, and then if I continue to save, my wife and I can take that nice vacation.* But that young family has discovered you cannot outgive God and it is more blessed to give than to receive.

Our church has also experienced the joy of giving. We have had four special offerings for new buildings over the past fifteen years, and each time, when the totals are announced, everyone has rejoiced and celebrated. The most dramatic incident occurred about twelve years ago when we came to our congregation just a few months after raising more than a million dollars to build our present building. Because of a rise in construction costs, we were going to need four hundred thousand dollars more than we had originally anticipated to complete the project. We decided to have a special offering, and people again sacrificed. We heard stories of people canceling vacations, taking on extra work, selling boats and sports cars, and postponing retirement so they could give more to the church.

When the total was announced at a Sunday night service, we had raised about three hundred forty thousand dollars, just sixty thousand short of our goal. We rejoiced and celebrated.

But I will never forget what happened next. You must understand that our church is very reserved. People don't speak out from the pews. Ever. The wildest thing that ever happens in our church is spontaneous clapping during an upbeat Southern gospel song. After we applauded the announcement of our total, our song leader was about to start another song when Emory Cockerham, an older gentleman who had never spoken out in our church before, walked up to the song leader. (Remember, *no* one had, and Emory was the least likely one to do so.) "Can I say something?" he asked.

"Well, I guess," our song leader said a bit reluctantly and handed him the microphone.

Emory said, "You know, that was a great offering, but it didn't quite reach the goal. That's not like us. We were so close I think we ought to pass the hat again tonight and see if we can reach the goal."

I headed for the front, preparing to say, "That's a fine idea, but I think we should just rejoice in how God has blessed us, and if you want to give additionally, you can see our building chairman afterward."

But before I could get to the microphone, Jack Coffee, the building chairman, beat me to it. He said, "I think that's a great idea, Emory! We don't have to start making our payments till January 1, so if you want to make pledges tonight, effective January 1, to help us reach that goal, you can do that. Ushers, get the offering plates."

By that time it was too late. I couldn't do anything about it. They passed the plate again and went off to count the second offering. We sang a few more hymns and waited for the announcement.

About fifteen minutes later, the counting crew came back in and announced that we had pledged an additional seventy-five thousand dollars, including sixteen thousand given in cash! I don't know who carries that much money around on Sunday nights, but we've done a lot more Sunday night offerings since then!

When the announcement was made, the congregation exploded from their seats. People were cheering, giving each other high-fives. I saw one of the elders and one of my sons standing on the pew above the crowd with their fists in the air!

Many members of our congregation have discovered it is more blessed to give than to receive. They have put off retirement, stayed in a smaller house, sold a second car, or given up vacations so they can give to furthering the kingdom of God. But as encouraging as these commitments are, they are not the largest or most influential gifts. One single mother of three teenagers gave her testimony before thousands of people one Sunday morning just before our commitment day. She said, "Because my husband left me and doesn't assist me, I have nothing to give to this program. But my children and I have agreed together that we will pray every day for God's blessing on you and this church as you give. But during our discussion, we determined there was something we could give. We have cable television. We decided we will give that up for the next three years, and that will be the amount we donate toward this project."

Jesus said that the woman who gave her last two mites gave more than all the rich men because she gave all that she had while the others had given out of their abundance. I know that single mom gave more than anyone.

The biggest challenges in life often produce the biggest rewards. It's difficult for us to give up our money. But God promises us a generous return on our investment, blessings beyond measure, and joy beyond comprehension, if we will be generous with what he has given us. I challenge you to discover the joy that can be yours when you give it away.

NOTES

CHAPTER ONE: MONEY IS NOT THE ROOT OF ALL EVIL

1. "Tyson: I should get more than $30 million a fight," *Chicago Tribune*, 23 March 1996, and "Tyson Replaces Jordan at Top," *Chicago Tribune*, 2 December 1996.

2. Rousas J. Rushdoony, *The Institutes of Biblical Law* (Nutley, N.J.: The Craig Press, 1973), 451.

CHAPTER TWO: IS WORK A CURSE?

1. Doug Sherman and William Hendricks, *Your Work Matters to God* (Colorado Springs: NavPress, 1987), 7, 77, 87.

2. Bill Hybels, *Christians in the Marketplace* (Wheaton: Victor Books, 1982), 12.

CHAPTER THREE: THE SUCCESS TRAP

1. Julie Connelly, "The Trophy Wife Is Back with Brains," *Fortune*, 3 April 1995, 102.

2. H. H. Lemmel, "Turn Your Eyes upon Jesus," (Nashville: Benson Music Publishing, 1922, renewed 1950).

CHAPTER FOUR: THE COMPARISON TRAP

1. Harrison Rainie with Margaret Loftus and Mark Madden, "The State of Greed," *US News & World Report*, 17 June 1996, 62.

CHAPTER FIVE: FOUR WAYS TO OVERCOME THE TRAPS

1. David E. Pitt, "Just a Paper Loss, the Richest Say," *New York Times*, 21 October 1987, 6.

2. Rainie, "The State of Greed," 64.

CHAPTER SIX: HAVE YOU FALLEN INTO THE DEBT
TRAP?

1. Larry Burkett, *Victory over Debt: Rediscovering Financial Freedom* (Chicago: Northfield Publishing, 1992), 4.

2. Ron and Judy Blue, *Money Matters for Parents and Their Kids* (Nashville: Thomas Nelson Publishers, Oliver-Nelson Books, 1988), 20.

3. "The American Way of Buying: Portrait of a Young Consumer as Wastrel," *Wall Street Journal,* 3 October 1989.

4. *Final Report of the Attorney General's Commission on Pornography* (Nashville: Rutledge Hill Press, 1986), 281, 289–90.

5. "To Verify," *Leadership Journal* 17, no. 3 (Summer 1996): 69.

6. First United Methodist Church paper, Newport Richey, Florida.

7. Burkett, *Victory over Debt,* 7, 71–72.

8. Ron Blue, *The Debt Squeeze* (Colorado Springs: Focus on the Family, 1989), 96, 102.

9. *Los Angeles Times,* 19 September 1996.

CHAPTER SEVEN: LESSONS LEARNED IN A PIGPEN

1. Austin Pryor, *Sound Mind Investing Newsletter* 3, no. 4 (April 1992): 42. Used by permission.

CHAPTER EIGHT: THE KEYS TO WISE SPENDING

1. Richard Case, Paul Meier, and Frank Minirth, *The Money Diet* (Grand Rapids, Mich.: Fleming H. Revell, 1995), 38.

2. Randy Alcorn, as quoted in *Sound Mind Investing Newsletter* 7, no. 7 (July 1996): 103.

3. *Guinness Book of World Records,* special ed. (New York: Sterling Publishing, 1988), 236–37.

4. Marc Eisenson, *A Banker's Secret* (Elizaville, N.Y.: Good Advice Press, 1989), 64.

5. Anthony Campolo, *The Kingdom of God Is a Party* (Dallas: Word Publishing, Inc., 1990), 17.

6. Austin Pryor, *Sound Mind Investing* (Chicago: Moody Press, 1996), 57–58.

7. Ibid., 393.

8. Ibid., 196–98.

CHAPTER NINE: CAN YOU SAVE TOO MUCH?

1. *Guiness Book of World Records,* 326.

2. Adam Platt, "The Titans of Tightwad," *Forbes,* 20 November 1995, 136–44.

3. Elizabeth Cheney, "Overheard in an Orchard," *The Best Loved Religious Poems* (Grand Rapids, Mich.: Fleming H. Revell, 1933), 215.

4. Maureen Dowd, "Sharing the Wealth," *New York Times,* 22 August 1996, 25.

CHAPTER TEN: THE WISEST INVESTMENTS

1. Max Lucado, *And the Angels Were Silent* (Portland, Ore.: Multnomah Press, 1992), 128–29.

CHAPTER ELEVEN: TEST GOD IN THIS

1. Bob Benson, *See You at the House* (Nashville: Thomas Nelson Publishers, Generoux Nelson, 1989), 102.

2. Benjamin J. Stein, *The American Spectator* as quoted in *Reader's Digest,* October 1996, 36.